HOW TO CONTACT THE SPACE PEOPLE

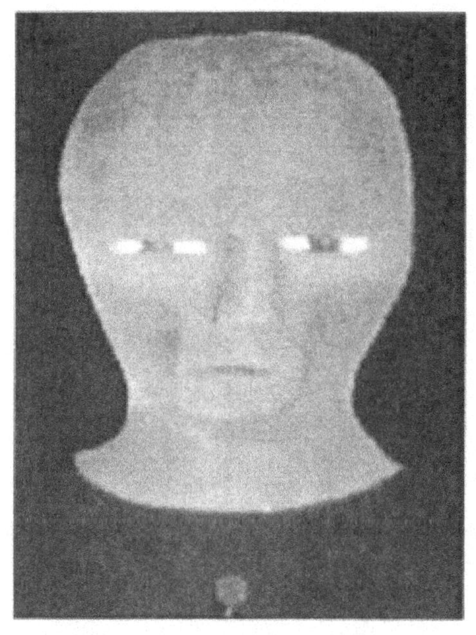

Ted Owens

Global Communications

HOW TO CONTACT

SPACE PEOPLE

By TED OWENS

Title Page Image:
One of the Space Intelligences

Special Reprint

With Additional Material By
Timothy Green Beckley
Otto Binder
Jeffrey Mishlove Ph.D.

ISBN : 1-60611-001-2
EAN : 978-1-60611-001-0

Editorial Direction by Timothy Green Beckley
Publishers Consultant Carol Ann Rodriguez
Cover Graphics by Tim Swartz

Global Communications,
Box 753, New Brunswick, NJ 08903

HOW TO CONTACT THE SPACE PEOPLE

Telepathic Communication With ETs Now Possible With Your Free Ted Owens "SI Disc"

Do The Saucer Intelligence Control Our Weather? Our Civilizations? Our Very Lives With Their Incredible Advanced Science?

Ted Owens

SPECIAL OFFER FROM THE PUBLISHER!

FREE BONUS SI DISC

All those buying a copy of *HOW TO CONTACT THE SPACE PEOPLE* are eligible to receive a free SI Disc as used by Ted Owens to contact the space people.

Email us with your full name and mailing address:
mrufo8@hotmail.com

OR, send a letter with your name and mailing address to:

Tim Beckley, Publisher
Inner Light Publications
Box 753
New Brunswick, NJ. 08903

You can also call our 24-hour hotline. Leave a message with your full name and mailing address: 732-602-3407

REQUEST YOUR FREE SI DISC AND PLEASE LET US KNOW WHERE YOU OBTAINED A COPY OF THE BOOK.

CONTENTS

Ted Owens

THE 'INCREDIBLE' TED OWENS

INTRODUCTION TO 2008 EDITION OF *HOW TO CONTACT THE SPACE PEOPLE*

By Timothy Green Beckley

Ted Owens and I were buddies.

Not only did he fill my mailbox with testimonials about his supernormal powers, but we also hung out in the hood.

The "hood" being the mean streets of New York City during the 1970s. Now a good number of you may assume that Ted Owens was some sort of slick hustler out to make a quick buck, or at least trying to obtain fame and "fortune" among his friends.

One thing I have to say is that throughout the years I stayed in touch with Ted, I never knew him to make anything we could calculate as a "quick buck," though Ted had told me that his friends the SI's had once led him to a nice size treasure, which is something they have done for others throughout the years.

Owens WAS another type of hustler. He had once told me he was known as a pretty good pool shark, and, noting that I claimed talents on the billiard table, we more than once took each other on, pool cue in hand.

Ted Owens

As I recall, when it came to playing Eight Ball, we were about equal. But when it came to paranormal powers, Ted Owens far surpassed my little bittie attempts at finding lost objects and the one or two out of body experiences I underwent as a child.

As you read this book you will be offered up some incredible events, far beyond the normal range of contactee experiences. What Ted Owens makes claim to is mind boggling. I always thought of him as sort of the Voodoo man of UFOlogy, for not only does Owens state matter-of-factly that he is in constant touch with these ETs he identifies as the Space Intelligence, he maintains that they not only protect him from harm, but also offer up any number of ways to correct our attitude toward them and their plans for Planet Earth.

Frankly, there is no middle ground with Ted Owens and his SI's. If you do them "right" there is no end to what they can do for you. If, on the other hand, you "wrong" them in some why, they will get even ... perhaps make your life more difficult than might be expected, or at least give a kick in the butt to your favorite sports team.

Though deceased now for a number of years, the predictions Ted made before his death were uncanny. He foretold major events, including blackouts, weeks before they occurred. He always kept meticulous records and insisted it was the SI's who were making these things happen and not any sort of psychokinetic powers he might possess.

Others who have researched Ted's "talents" would go out of their way to propose other solutions to what was apparently occurring all around him

In the end, it's your decision to make. We have included in his words all that he had to say as published in his original manuscript, issued by my old friend Gray Barker of Saucerian Press fame. We have also included the thinking of Otto Binder, who was sort of Ted's unofficial biographer and wrote about him several times in the popular men's magazine of the period known as *Saga*. Then there is Ph.D Jeffrey Mishlove, whose manuscript *PK*

MAN served as his doctoral diploma in parapsychology from UC Berkeley. I am the first to admit that Meshlove's research is more in-depth than I could ever claim to equal on the subject of Ted Owens. Later on, at the end of the book, we make his work available for those who want to access more detail regarding Ted's life and claims.

But above all else, we are also including one of the most important artifacts in UFO contact-dom, the famous SI Disc which Ted offered to the original readers of his work. We want you to have a disc all your own. All we ask is that you report any paranormal occurrences attributed to the disc directly to us. Don't go out and attempt to cause thunderstorms unless you live in a drought area. Don't use it to attack your enemies or to do them harm. Most importantly, don't try to turn the Earth on its axis in order to slow down global warming.

Remember, Ted Owens may have thought he was akin to Moses, but you probably aren't!

In any case, enjoy the book you are now digging into. There is a lot of valuable information in these pages. I am pleased to present the Ted Owens story to you and allow you to make up your own mind as to his contact claims.

Timothy Green Beckley
MRUFO@webtv.net

Spokesman for the UFO's

By Otto Binder

Have we been sent-and ignored-messages from spacemen ?

Do the Saucer Intelligences control our weather, our civilization, our very lives with their incredibly advanced science ?

Has one man, Ted Owens, really been selected to "relay" their warnings and predictions ?

Do we have in our midst a

"SPOKESMAN" FOR THE UFO'S ?

By Otto O. Binder

A letter to Pres. Richard M. Nixon, dated July 30, 1969, read in part:

"The SI's told me that there is a plot already underway ... has been completely planned ... to kidnap you at your Key Biscayne residence (Florida). The 'bad guys' (Cubans) know how well protected you are ... but they are going to strike at night, by water ... with fast boats ... with a highly skilled commando group of 50-100 men."

The letter was signed,

Ted Owens, PK Man.

The Miami Herald on August 24, 1969-only three weeks later-carried the headline:

SPY PLOT SHATTERS PROSPECTS FOR RENEWING U.S. CUBA TIES.

After revealing that Fidel Castro's U.N. diplomats doubled as spies, the text stated:

"The U.S. public is likely to consider the recruitment of spies for a mission relating to Presidential security very much more seriously than guerrilla activities in a faraway land. There was, according to some reports, a James Bond touch to the recruitment plot ... These reports claimed the plan was to study President Nixon's movements at his Key Biscayne home, using scuba divers as part of the surveillance team."

On March 10, 1966, after years of drought in the Northeastern states, Ted Owens wrote to Pres. Lyndon Johnson:

"I have some very good news : from the UFO Intelligences ... to PK man ... to you. The SI's have decided to end the entire drought on the East Coast. In the days, weeks, and months to come there will be rain, rain, rain ... not just a little, not just 'above average', but phenomenal rain ..."

From the Philadelphia Enquirer of July 22, 1967:

"We were pleased to note ... the admission by the United States Weather Bureau ... that the drought which plagued the northeast corner of the country for the last six years, has ended."

After citing that abnormal rains had been reported all through the northeast during the spring and early summer, it was stated that New York's reservoirs "could hardly be fuller".

The year 1967 was also called the "year that had no spring" because it rained so much. The sunny days of blossoming flowers and awakening life were rare. The rainy spring led to an even wetter summer, as if nature was making up for the six years of drought all in one year.

How To Contact The Space People

On October 26, 1965, a telegram sent to George Clark, CIA, Washington, D.C., held this alarming statement:

"A rare warning. They (the SI's) will unleash a terrible catastrophe within 10 days."

Signed:

"PK man" (Owens).

A little more than 10 days passed without incident. But on November 9, 1965, the Big Blackout hit seven northeastern states and parts of Canada, plunging 30 million people into darkness. Without electrical power for up to 12 hours, the lights of entire cities flickered out, machines stopped, and TV and radio went off. Emergency measures were required to rescue people trapped in stalled elevators and subway trains. Hospitals switched on their own power generators for critical operations.

Was this what the telegram meant?

On the morning of November 14, 1969, the Apollo 12 was in the final stages of the countdown, ready for lift-off to man's second moon landing. North of Cape Kennedy, in Virginia Beach, Va., three prominent citizens (their signed and sworn affidavits are on file) heard Ted Owens state that lightning would strike either the pad or the spacecraft.

Seconds after the giant rocket roared into the overcast sky, the control crew at Cape Kennedy was alarmed to see a sudden drop-off of telemetered data from the spacecraft. Through an alternate voice-circuit, astronaut Charles Conrad told how lights had gone out within the spacecraft, adding:

"I don't know what happened. I'm not sure we didn't get hit by lightning."

The PK man had done - it again.

Ted Owens

More tragic was the prediction in a letter of March 4, 1968, sent by Ted Owens to government agencies, relaying a warning from the SI's of the "destruction of one or more highly-placed U.S. Government Officials -by - assassination." Within 12 weeks, Martin Luther King and Robert Kennedy were killed by assassins' bullets.

The above are only a few cases out of more than 200 document ed predictions and paranormal phenomena originated by Ted Owens.

Now, just who is this Ted Owens, the PK Man? He is a tall, broad shouldered man of 50, with a receding hairline, thin lips, penetrating brown eyes, and an IQ of 150. But that doesn't tell you who or what he really is. Let the man who knows him best do that, Ted Owens himself:

"I am the only human being alive able to communicate two ways with the SI's, and prove it. I'm the PK Man."

The SI's are Saucer (or Space) Intelligences. PK stands for "psychokinesis," the power to manipulate, move, or otherwise affect physical objects, through mental forces alone. The two are related. Ted Owens claims he gets his PK powers from the SI's.

It all began, says Owens, in 1965. In order to support his wife and three children, he had already "mastered 50 professions," a bewildering variety including lecturer, jazz drummer, magician, hypnotist, bodyguard, boxer, private investigator, office manager, fortune teller, teacher of auto suggestion, instructor in knife throwing, designer of jewelry, psychiatric secretary, lifeguard, and last (of this incomplete list) but hardly least - rainmaker.

He cheerfully admits he has no academic degree or official standing in the "establishment", yet it's a matter of record that he has an IQ of 150 (genius starts at 140), and for two years worked with Prof. J.B. Rhine at Duke University, in various ESP experiments. In a private gathering with Rhine and his wife, Louisa, plus friends, Owens startlingly demonstrated his PK powers by causing a scissors to whisk off a table and fly for several feet without being touched.

How To Contact The Space People

It all really began on that day in 1965 ... but let Ted Owens himself describe it (from his book-How to Contact Space People-Saucerian Publications, 1969):

"While living in Fort Worth, Tex., my daughter and I were driving in the country one night, when a cigar shaped UFO suddenly appeared at our left over a field, and came floating toward our car making no noise. It had red, white, blue, and green colors flaming vividly from it. Its nose was tilted down towards the ground. As we watched, it approached close to our car, then instantly vanished, just like a light turned off".

At first glance, this seems to merely be one of the many vivid, although common, saucer sightings. But it was far more than that for Ted Owens, as he wrote:

"From that day on, my life changed radically ... While in Fort Worth I gave my daughter, Lornie, several demonstrations of making lightning strike in certain areas during thundershowers. I was playfully experimenting with a theory I had on the practical application of PK or psychokinetic power, to nature's forces."

Notice the word "playfully". Owens was soon shocked to discover that his "playing" was real after his family had moved to Phoenix, Ariz., which at that time was in the midst of a bad drought.

"The idea to experiment with ESP for weather control came to me again, so I gathered my children together and showed them how I would make it storm. It did, so intensely that the city was declared a disaster area."

We can infer that Ted Owens was more amazed at his success than he admits, and a bit dubious of his presumed PK powers.

"To make sure that it was I who had brought this about, and not just a coincidence, I announced to my family we would make a series of storms-and I wrote to the local papers to that effect."

Owens was certainly gambling, for it would be the first publicized demonstration of his PK powers-if he had them. The results were astounding.

"It produced eight terrible, rocking thunderstorms complete with tremendous lightning displays, within a period of three weeks."

Owens has signed and notorized statements from his family that all this is true. Now all of Owens's doubts vanished.

"Electrified by my success, and knowing for certain that I had something, I wrote to government agencies and to many important people, but to no avail. No one would believe me. We moved then to Los Angeles, also in the middle of a drought, and I made some tremendous storms there."

This too is fully documented.

Owens was careful to document his apparent PK feats by telling various officials or prominent people what he proposed to do, then having them sign an affidavit before or after the event occurred on schedule. Some of these will be quoted later, in connection with more important events. But gradually, there came a greater revelation to Ted Owens...

"Now, I figured that somehow I had managed to contact the essence of the intelligence behind Nature herself."

This seemed to be so, because soon after, when Hurricane Cleo began roaring off the coast of Florida, Owens excitedly drew a rough map and told his family he would "control" the storm. He writes:

"To the amazement of my family, the hurricane followed my map to the letter!"

Now sure of himself, Owens then stuck his neck way out. In October 1966, he boldly announced to the Florida weather bureau exactly what he was going to do-"guide" Hurricane Inez north from Cuba instead of west as expected, then make it backtrack and hit the Florida coast when all the "experts" said it would go out to sea. Inez followed Owens' "schedule" to the hilt. Weathermen admitted it was "unorthodox" almost impossible.

Even more "impertinent" was Owens' notice to the Chief of the U.S. Hurricane Center in June 1967, saying that the SI would produce three simultaneous hurricanes. This had happened only four times before since 1886. In September of 1967, Hurricanes Beulah, Chloe, and Doris were all active on the same weekend, something that the weather bureau admitted was "unprecedented" in modem times.

Obviously, if he really had this power to turn and guide hurricanes, Owens could perform a great service for the country. He thereupon bombarded government officials in Washington with letters, telling them what he could do and offering his "anti-disaster" powers. Some men, like Clark of the CIA and Eastwood of NASA saw him in person, and admitted a strong interest in his claims, but the regret was, as Owens puts it-"no action". If they didn't consider him a harmless crackpot (he does not resemble one), they were apparently hamstrung in their attempts to reach their superiors.

Another big turn in Ted Owens' personal life came when he discovered that he had not, by himself, created or guided storms by some eerie contact with the "essence of the intelligence of Nature". It was some other intelligence, and he writes that, after moving to Washington, D.C., in 1965,

"I discovered for the first time it was not Nature, but the UFO Intelligences who I had been contacting, and who had been guiding me."

Owens had become aware of a "saucer flap" in the area, which was part of the great UFO wave of 1965-66. Then, quite unexpectedly, he received a message from the SI's telling him to inform the CIA that incredible magnetic phenomena would occur at the north and south poles.

After sending this "prediction" to CIA man Clark, Owens wrote:

Ted Owens

"On July 8 (1965) all the newspapers carried a startling story: FLYING SAUCER IS REPORTED OVER TWO SOUTH POLE BASES! This huge disc-shaped UFO was clearly seen and photographed by many scientists of several nations, and they reported that it created powerful electromagnetic (per Owens' prediction) forces on their instruments."

A bombshell burst in Ted Owens' mind...

"I found out, with a jolt, that what I had been dealing with ... were UFO Intelligences!"

From then on, relates the PK Man, he was able to mentally "tune in" these Space Intelligences at any time. They arranged between them a series of phenomena whereby Owens would "predict" something and the SI's would make it come true. In some cases, they did this by beefing up his PK powers and letting him work the deed. In other cases, the SI's would do the job directly, keeping Owens informed.

The result has been the 200-plus PK feats and incredible predictions-all apparently documented-that have flowed from Ted Owens during the past six years.

Let's establish one thing here and now: Ted Owens is not a wild-eyed "contactee". He has never met an ST face to face nor has he travelled in their ships; he has not been whisked to their far off Utopian world nor has he eaten their exotic foods.

Owens makes it quite plain, repeatedly, that he has only a mental contact with the SI's, that for some reason unknown even to Owens (as he himself freely admits) his brain is the ideal "receiving station" for SI telepathic messages, and most significantly, that he can "talk" directly to them on a two-way hookup. Owens believes that he is the only one on earth today with this remarkable ESP ability, and that in the past, perhaps only Edgar Cayce, Moses, and the wise men from some ancient civilizations had such direct SI contact.

How To Contact The Space People

Ted Owens variously calls himself a "go-between" for the SI's in their dealings, or attempted dealings, with mankind; their "mouthpiece", their "front", their human "relay station" for messages.

Owens constantly reiterates that he is not "responsible" for what the SI's do, even through his own PK powers, as they do all the planning and executing. Their purpose in all their paranormal doings, via Owens, is to prove their presence so that the authorities will listen to them (via Owens) and accept help. Whatever seeming "disasters" Ted Owens has been connected with, in the following accounts, the SI's claim they are here on earth to prevent a greater calamity. We will examine the motivations of the SI's more fully later on.

Although Ted Owens has never been a UFOlogist or been active in the UFO field in any way, his special and personal relationship with the Saucer Intelligences has shed light on certain UFO phenomena in general.

EM-effects.

In answer to the question

Why do flying saucers affect cars and electrical instruments when they come close?

Owens says:

"I'm glad you asked that, because the SI's just recently explained it to me ... When they come into an area they want to investigate they throw out a 'net', just like a fisherman throws his net overboard ... They ex tend an electromagnetic net all around them that will trap and stop all power in that. area in order to keep anybody from being able to communicate with humans outside the SI net, to radio for help, or to radio for airplane interference (from Air Force bases)... Why don't Forest Rangers, who take care of our national forests, shoot bears and animals instead of tranquillizing them and tagging them? The SI's could actually destroy all humans in that area if they wanted, instead of throwing out a tranquillizing, power-stopping electromagnetic net."

This implies (perhaps the most the SI's have revealed to Owens) that those landings which exhibit EM-effects are for the purpose of "tranquillizing" and "tagging" certain human specimens. This activity of course is not seen or reported in saucer sightings. We actually know little about the strange activities the SI's carry on when they mingle with humans.

Falls from the sky. Though not always directly connected with sightings of UFOs, objects falling from the sky have been a riddle all through history. Huge falls of fish, toads, chunks of meat, blood-almost anything. Hundreds of these reports were collected by Charles Fort and these occurrences still continue in modern times. Sometimes they happen just after a UFO has flown over. And one particular substance-angel hair, a mass of odd fibbers-has often been directly seen falling from a UFO.

In answer to a question about a recent report of flesh and blood falling from the sky, and whether the SI's had anything to do with it, Owens provides a fascinating answer:

"I don't think the flesh and blood fell from the sky. I think the flesh and blood fell out of the other dimension (from which the SI's come). In all the cases where I have read of a shower of fish or rocks falling from the sky, I believe it is caused by the SI's opening a crack in their dimension to let their craft in or out."

Owens gives a more specific example in which he supposes that a UFO is rising out of the water and

"they see people on the bank of the lake or the ocean, so they switch off into another dimension. But as they have come up out of the water, their power (EM field) might draw fish up with them, or rocks, or even people. When they switch on again into this (Earth) dimension (a moment later), in a different area than before, perhaps clear across the world, then those same fish or rocks or people-or parts of people-come back out with them and shower down."

A rather gruesome explanation as to how flesh and blood might fall from the sky. Ruthless? Cruel? But if our spacecraft some day land on another world and the scheduled time for take-off comes, would the astronauts turn off their rockets just because a few natives or animals were within the blast area and might get burned to death?

"Monster-men" and "Humanoids".

Owens admitted he knew very little about these creatures so often seen during saucer landings. But he ventured this concept, which should interest Coral Lorenzen, who in one of her books advanced the same theory. She wrote that people saw humanoids or "hairy dwarfs" step out of saucers to collect plants or rocks. Owens said:

"Yes, these are the SI's pets, which collect samples from earth for the SI's. Just as we use chimpanzees or porpoises, cats and dogs and horses, etc., to do the work for us. But for what purpose they want these samples, I don't really know."

He says the SI's do not consult him on weighty matters, nor include him in master conferences concerning Earth's fate. His messages from them are strictly limited to the PK duties he is to perform. This should make most of us pause before calling this man a charlatan or self-deluded kook. Kooks and crackpots, as everyone knows, always place themselves one step below God (if they're modest) and share his omniscience.

Various reporters, columnists, and other influential people (who will be named below) have said the PK Man's remarkable predictions might be coincidence or luck, but not likely. The facts seem to speak for themselves.

Let's look at one of Owens' most sensational PK feats.

Owens once said to a sports writer:

"Sports is a superficial thing. But it's an excellent way to demonstrate the SI's power over a small group of men."

Owens demonstrated the truth of his dictum by creating havoc with two Philadelphia sports teams, the Eagles of the National Football League and the 76'ers of pro basketball. Why he chose Philadelphia is a question that remains unanswered.

He wrote to a dozen sports writers before the 1968 season opened, that he "would take the Eagles apart with PK," and absolutely crush their chances for the championship. He promised that the Eagles would have at least 20 injuries and would lose more games than they won.

The Eagles had 30 injuries that season and lost 11 games in a row.

That this was totally unexpected and almost weirdly unbelievable is seen from these expressions and quotes in the columns of sports writers: "Injury curse hits Eagles" ... "Talk of jinxes and voodoo" ... "The bewitched Eagles" ... "Some whammy working on the team".

Writer Stan Hochman wrote in the Philadelphia Daily News, September 30, 1968, after taking Owens to an Eagles' game,

"I figured I'd pin him (Owens) down as to his claims of hexing the team."

"When the Eagles scored and went ahead 3-0, Owens said, 'The SI's are going to have to get Woodeshick. Get him out of the game.'"

"Woodeshick was the team's star. A brawl began between two other players and suddenly there was Woodeshick out there ... They threw him out of the game for fighting ... The game even got stranger in the third quarter..."

After a fumble, four Eagles were unable to pick up the ball and the Cowboys took possession. The Eagles lost the game.

In another column Stan Hochman wrote:

"For a while, Ted Owens was content to cause rainstorms where there had been no rain for six years. He did work up that satisfying power blackout in 1967 (June) when he snuffed out the light for the East Coast. But . nobody came clamoring after Ted Owens to buy his cloud-bursting, light-snuffing services."

Hochman then recited the incredible roster of injuries, freak plays, and hard-luck breaks that overwhelmed the Eagles during the 1968 exhibition season. (They were to continue throughout the regular season). Without endorsing Ted Owens' claims, Hochman reiterated that everything that had happened to the Eagles was foretold by the PK Man and published.

Paid attendance to the Eagles' games naturally fell off and Jerry Wolman the team's owner, filed bankruptcy.

Was it all a fluke? Were the Eagles destined to flop on their faces in 1968 without the intervention of the PK Man's alleged powers? Owens tested himself again in pro-basketball. On April 23, 1968, a prominent lawyer signed a statement that Owens had predicted the Philadelphia 76'ers would lose their play-off games with the Boston Celtics, and that the 76'ers would miss their shots to an incredible degree.

George Kiseda, sports writer: "76'ers shooting is off ... They might as well have been trying to put a medicine ball in a teacup." Sam Jones of the Celtics was quoted as saying: "I don't think (our) defense is what's beaten them. They're just missing shots." Again a sports writer:

"The 76'ers simply couldn't put the ball in the basket."

The strange part was that the 76'ers were famed as a "sharp shooting" team. The payoff, as another sports writer put it:

"They went blind from the floor ... and suffered a 122-104 crushing. Back to Boston Wednesday and the blindness continued . : . They shot apathetic 18-for-68 and the Celtics had little trouble in slipping away with a 114-106 win that evened it all at 3-3 (games)."

The Celtics, the underdogs, went on to win the play-offs, the first team even to come from behind and win. Keeping all the above extraordinary factors in mind, either the laws of chance went completely haywire-or the awesome forces exerted by the PK Mann fulfilled his threatening prophecy. Take your pick..

Some of his more recent predictions have been startlingly fulfilled according to the available evidence.

On February 10, 1970, Owens was interviewed by Lawrence Maddry of the Virginian-Pilot, Virginia Beach, Va. Picking a distant state, Owens predicted that a flying saucer would be sighted over the Brewer-Bangor area of Maine, and that some sort of power failure would occur at the same time. The deadline was two weeks but after only one week headlines from the Bangor area press screamed of a flying saucer sighting; there was also the story of one witnesses' car whose battery went dead.

During the interview, Maddry had asked:

"Well, Mr. Owens. What do you think will happen while you're here?"

"I look for some kind of power failure,"

he said. When the reporter went out to start his car, he had a dead battery. Maddry's column dryly says-

"Informed of this, Owens' eyes rolled slightly in their sockets ... 'Hmm, they must be very close.'"

In early January 1970 Owens handed a letter to a reporter stating that he would make one or more earthquakes for the reporter's paper on January 22nd... On that date earthquakes were reported in Berkeley, Calif., and in Japan. In fact, six earthquakes were reported from January 22nd to February 12th, which Owens explains as the SI's being unable to control the "echo" earthquakes that resulted from those of January 22nd.

More impressive is Owens' bold statement to Lawrence Maddry and other reporters that the SI's would carry on a "private war" with Pan American Airways and that the Atlantic Ocean would become a "no man's land" for their giant 747 superliners.

Two days later a Pan Am-747 left Puerto Rico, became disabled over the Atlantic and had to return to the airfield. The next day a 747 leaving London had to jettison fuel and also return to base. The following day a 747 crashed on the runway at Stockton, California.

Is that guessing-or knowing?

There is much more to tell about Ted Owens that could not be included here but will be included later. To be covered will be Owens' cases of PK healing, which are far fewer than those of the renowned Edgar Cayce but no less astounding. Also an intriguing explanation of who and what the SI's are, how many UFOs they have, how they operate, and what the fate of Earth will be if their (SI's) battle against the evil OIs (Other Intelligences) does not succeed.

Then, there is the strange way the SI's communicate with Owens, involving "Tweeter and Twitter", two amazing SI creatures.

Let us conclude with one more prediction by Ted Owens-which is really a message from the SI's as to their future plans. It should make all true UFOlogists sit up and take notice. The written-out and signed prediction is dated February 13, 1970, and was confirmed to me in another letter a week later. Here it is, verbatim:

"This time the experiment (of the SI's) will not be confined to just one country ... it will be a worldwide demonstration of UFO power! As of this date I am contacting the SI's and asking them to activate a special apparatus they have ... to control weather ... on a worldwide scale! The object: to prove the existence of the SI's, and their ability to receive communications from me. The objective: to cause violent weather worldwide, from this day on, throughout the entire summer coming up in 1970."

"Not only that. But for the SI's 'signature' to this, they will appear in great numbers, here, there and everywhere."

"In short, you are now going to be privy to one of the greatest shows ever put on, on this earth. And it will be put on by the UFO

Intelligences, using their great powers. And these powers will issue forth from the Bermuda Triangle and the Devil's Triangle in the Pacific, I am positive."

Well, there you have it. Ted Owens has more-or-less staked his reputation on this direct prediction. If, when you read this, the world is being plagued by violent storms and disasters, and if there is also the greatest wave of UFO saucer sightings and landings in history, it could be coincidence.

Or it could be the word of Ted Owens, PK Man, coming true.

Ted Owens' past record-200 documented predictions and paranormal phenomena-is indisputable testimony of the man's unique role as a "go-between" for the Space Intelligences. For instance, in June 1967 he notified the U.S. Hurricane Center that the SI's would produce three simultaneous hurricanes. This had happened only four times before since 1886. In September 1967, Hurricanes Beulah, Chloe, and Doris were all active on the same weekend, something that the weather bureau admitted was "unprecedented" in modern times!

Jeffrey Mishlove, PhD

President, Intuition Network -- a nonprofit organization dedicated to helping create a world in which all people are encouraged to cultivate their inner, intuitive resources

Jeffrey Mishlove, PhD, president of the Intuition Network, has been a writer, television host and producer, psychotherapist, businessman and researcher of extraordinary human capacities and psychic abilities. His newest publication, an ebook, is Jeffrey Mishlove's Handbook for Contestants in CNBC's 2007 Million Dollar Portfolio Challenge.

Jeff Mishlove in 2004 atop Turtlehead Peak in the Red Rock National Conservation Area near his southern Nevada home

Since 1988, Jeff's weekly television program, Thinking Allowed, has been shown throughout the United States. During this period he has conducted hundreds of interviews with leading figures in psychology, philosophy, science, health and spirituality. It is currently shown throughout North America on the Wisdom Channel -- and is also streamed on the internet via the Wisdom Media Group.

Jeff holds a unique doctoral diploma in "Parapsychology" from the University of California at Berkeley. Awarded in 1980, it remains the only doctoral diploma in parapsychology ever awarded by an accredited, American university. He currently serves as Dean of Programs for the newly created University of Philosophical Research affiliated with the Philosophical Research Society of Los Angeles. This unique college program offers masters degrees in consciousness studies and transformational psychology.

In 1999, Jeff wrote a book called The PK Man: A True Story of Mind Over Matter. He is author of three previous books. The Roots of Consciousness: Psychic Exploration Through History, Science and Experience was originally published in 1975 by Random House. Since then it has been widely used as a college text for introductory courses in consciousness exploration. A second, revised edition was published in 1993 by Council Oak Books of Tulsa, OK. His second book, Psi Development Systems, based on his doctoral dissertation was released in 1983 as a Ballantine paperback. It is an evaluation of ancient and modern methods for training extrasensory abilities. His third book, Thinking Allowed, released by Council Oak Books, is a collection of thirty-two interviews from his television series.

Jeff is past-president of the California Society for Psychical Study and past-vice-president of the Association for Humanistic Psychology. In 2001, the Association presented him with its "Pathfinder Award" for his outstanding contributions to the field of consciousness exploration. He is currently a member of the American Psychological Association and the Parapsychological Association.

Jeff also serves as Executive Director of two management consulting and training companies, TMI US and Branded Customer Service.

Visit Mishlove.Com and see "Rainbow YinYang" artwork created by Jeff Mishlove.

'VIRTUAL U'

WITH DR. JEFFREY MISHLOVE

Transcribed by Joyce Rosenfield

Jeffrey Mishlove: Hello, and welcome! This is Jeffrey Mishlove, host of Virtual U. Our conversation today is going to focus in on one of the most fascinating adventures of my entire life. We're going to explore the subject of contacting Space Intelligence. And this is an adventure, and research project, in which I was engaged for over 10 years, between 1976 and 1987.

I was involved in the study of a most unusual individual, a man named Ted Owens, author of the book, How to Contact Space People, a very obscure book published by Saucerian Press in 1969.

How did I meet this man? And what were his powers? The story will unfold over the coming hours of this edition of *Virtual U*. It is a story about a most unusual man, a man larger than life, a man whose powers were of shamanistic proportions, although I regard him as something like an American folk hero, a Paul Bunyan or a Pecos Bill type!

I swear to you, everything that I am presenting in this program is true. You're going to hear things that are unbelievable, but they are true, and I have the documentation to prove it.

The story of Ted Owens would be interesting if it were just another "Oh, wow!" story. We could sit around the campfire and tell stories like this. But it has profound implications for our human potential. For our self-awareness.

The story begins in 1976 when I was a graduate student at the University of California at Berkeley, studying parapsychology. At that time I was very interested in "Remote Viewing", a clairvoyant procedure that was being developed at the Stanford Research Institute, now known as SRI International, by two physicists there,

Ted Owens

Russell Targ and Hal Puthoff, both of whom have become very prominent in the field of physics and in the field of parapsychology.

Back in 1976 I went to visit them and learn about Remote Viewing. It was at that time that they gave me their very extensive files on Ted Owens and encouraged me to follow his career, and to initiate a research project of my own into the remarkable work that he was doing then. And I did.

And let me tell you why I thought it was such an important case to follow. You see, Puthoff and Targ had achieved a lot of public prominence in the early 1970's for their research with the Israeli psychic Uri Geller. Uri Geller, many of you will know, had achieved a lot of fame and notoriety because he ostensibly had psychokinetic powers, mind over matter powers, and he was bending spoons and stopping watches. People would see him on television and they would discover sometimes that spoons would start bending in their own homes, and actually around the world, it was quite a phenomenon.

Hundreds of thousands of people began recording metal-bending, spoon-bending, simply from watching Uri Geller on television. And people were holding "spoon-bending parties"! And it even became a fad within the military. It was quite exciting.

I knew about these things. I was in on it because I had sponsored Uri Geller's first major public appearance back in 1973 on the University of California campus at Berkeley.

I was a graduate student at Berkeley and I was producing radio programs back then, and organizing events like this. So I was in the middle of all this excitement.

Puthoff and Targ, being serious scientists working at a major military-industrial think tank, had by that time, in 1976, had become burnt out with the publicity and the controversy surrounding Uri Geller. Hopefully, we'll spend another program and really go into depth about the Geller phenomenon, and perhaps we'll even have Uri Geller as a guest on this program. He's been an acquaintance of mine for over twenty-five years, and there are many interesting things that could be said about him.

But for now, simply let me say that Puthoff and Targ didn't feel that they could handle another controversial psychic.

So when Ted Owens contacted them and said, "Why are you guys wasting your time with Uri Geller? I'm the world's greatest psychic!" Well, they felt they simply didn't want to get involved. They ignored him.

His contacts, however, went on for some time, over a period of weeks, months, perhaps even years, and he kept writing to them and badgering them to send him money to work as a research subject.

One day, in February of 1976, Owen sent Puthoff and Targ a letter. His letter read, Look, you guys, just to prove to you that I am indeed the world's greatest psychic, I am going to end the drought that is now plaguing you in California. And indeed there was a very serious drought that was going on at that time. He said, I will make it rain and snow and sleet and hail. You will have all sorts of bizarre weather going on, and there will be power blackouts, and there will be UFO sightings. And your local newspaper is going to run a front-page story proclaiming that the drought is over.

Within three days all of these things happened.

I have the article that was published in the Palo Alto *Times*, the local newspaper down there near SRI, Stanford Research Institute in Menlo Park, California. The article proclaims:

"Rare Snowfall Ends Drought". Of course many of you listeners now are all over the country, so you may not appreciate that snow in the San Francisco area is a very rare phenomenon -- maybe once every 15 or 20 years do we get snow.

So Puthoff and Targ were impressed. They sent a postcard to Ted Owens congratulating him on his successful prediction. He immediately sent a letter back to them and he said, in effect, "Hell, no! I caused it!"

It was at point, within a few weeks, I had visited SRI and was meeting with Puthoff and Targ, and it was then they said, "Jeffrey, please take this case off of our hands! We don't know what to do. We don't want to do anything, but somebody should look into it -- a promising young graduate student like yourself, who doesn't have a major career already on the line that could be ruined because of controversy and publicity!"

So I looked into the case. They gave me stacks and stacks, about six inches thick, of their files, including many, many letters that they had received from Ted Owens, documenting similar demonstrations.

It turned out at that time, there was a magazine published in San Francisco called Psychic Magazine. It later became New Realities and I think has subsequently gone out of business, but Psychic Magazine published a little news clip: Puthoff and Targ had talked to James Bolen, the Editor. His wife, Jean Shinoda Bolen, is the prominent Jungian therapist, the woman who wrote the books, "Goddesses in Every Woman", "Gods in Every Man". But James Bolen was the publisher of *Psychic* Magazine at that time.

He ran a little news story about this fellow, Ted Owens, who had successfully (apparently) ended the California drought. Psychic Magazine went around the world and it was read in England, because in 1976 there was a drought also going on in London, in England. It was so bad, in fact, that in some of the outlying towns, away from London, the only water available had to be brought in by truck!

The British, that summer, were hosting a Conference on Parapsychology. I was attending it. By "coincidence" they had invited Ted Owens to attend the same event, in the hope that he would also end the drought that was there. That drought was so bad that when I came to London, my friends told me, "Jeffrey, would you like to have your picture taken on the front page of the London *Times*. It's no problem. All you have to do is go down to Piccadilly Circus carrying an umbrella! People will think it's so strange, they'll take your picture and put it in the newspaper!"

There was just no rain at all. It was dry! But the day Ted Owens arrived in England, it began to rain and rain and rain, and there were power blackouts that also shut down the whole London subway-system, and within I think a matter of weeks, the London Times proclaimed that the drought was officially over, within a short time, although when I first arrived in London, the newspaper said "No End in Sight, for the Drought".

So I had now had two relatively convincing experiences that I could attest to, in which Owens in one way or another, seemed to be involved in suddenly and unexpectedly ending a drought.

I didn't know whether he had caused these phenomena, or had predicted these phenomena, or whether it was a coincidence, or whether perhaps it was simply a statistical fluke or maybe it wasn't even that! Maybe it was just happenstance, but my curiosity was aroused, and I made a point of meeting Ted Owens.

We actually became good friends. He was a Speaker at the London Parascience Conference held at Birkbeck College at the University of London -- a very prestigious scientific institution, and many physicists and well-known scientists and writers were at that event, when Ted Owens spoke.

He had a large white beard. He looked like Santa Claus, and he spoke in a very booming, articulate voice. He was a Member of MENSA, the organization of people with high IQ's. And yet there was something peculiar about this man.

He came into the auditorium carrying a toy wagon, and stacked in that toy wagon, about two feet high, were piles and piles of paper, and he claimed that he was the agent of the UFO's. He was their Ambassador, their Emissary, and he had come to Earth, or they had empowered him, by operating on his brain, and they had authorized him to perform miraculous feats to end the droughts, and to do wonderful things for people on Earth, in order to convince the people on Earth of his connection with the aliens and his powers!

And frankly, the audience laughed at him. They couldn't take him seriously. It just seemed too absurd, too ridiculous. That's when I stepped in, because I stood up and talked about what I had observed and known about in California. And I became his friend, and what followed from that friendship I will present after these messages.

[Segment Two follows]

Jeffrey Mishlove: I'm Jeffrey Mishlove, host of *Virtual U*, back again, talking about my adventures with Ted Owens and the Space Intelligences. In our first Segment, I described how I met Ted Owens at the Parascience Conference in August, 1976, Birkbeck College, University of London, and how he had already by then, established a reputation for having extraordinary psychokinetic abilities.

He even called himself PK Man, meaning the Psychokinesis Man, the man who had powers of mind over matter. And he also called himself The UFO Prophet.

When he stood up at the Parascience Conference to speak, people thought of him as being a highly inappropriate individual, and I have to say, that stigma followed him throughout his career. People thought that the man was an egotist, that he was brash, and although he was brilliant, a member of MENSA, he really didn't have an advanced educational degree.

He was more working-class in his vocabulary, in his mentality, and he seemed very much out of place at a scientific gathering, talking in his booming voice about how he was the Ambassador of the Aliens! Polite society was simply not ready for that in 1976, and I doubt that they're ready for that yet!

Then when he carried his toy wagon stacked high with papers which he claimed documented his feats, well, the whole thing seemed almost like the man was psychotic. I think there were people in that audience who were willing to dismiss him as a nut case. And there were people in the audience who were willing to dismiss him simply as being an arrogant egotist. And there were people in the audience willing to dismiss it largely because they were incapable of integrating what he was saying.

That was the difficulty throughout his whole career.

I befriended him by standing up for him at that meeting and telling people what I personally was aware of with regard to ending the drought in February, 1975, at the San Francisco Bay Area. And I think the audience quieted down a little bit. They began to listen to him.

After that talk, Ted Owens came up to me. I was doing radio interviews at the time, and I actually interviewed him for my program on KPFA Radio in Berkeley. I had a tape-recorder with me then, and we became friends.

We were talking, and he noticed that I had a little ceramic pin that I wore on my jacket. It was given to me by my girl-friend back then, before I left for Europe. It was a picture of what I took to be the Planet Saturn, with a rainbow behind it. A lovely New Age kind of design, and Ted Owens looked at that and he said to me, "You know, that's the Rainbow UFO."

He said, "Do you know that every day I meditate on the Rainbow UFO." He said, "Jeffrey, I'd really love it if you would make a gift to me of that pin. It would mean so much to me."

Gosh, I thought, wait a minute! That's from my girl-friend! But there was Ted Owens, the UFO Prophet, asking for it, and I did. I took it off my jacket and gave it to him. My relationship with my girl-friend really didn't last too much longer, but that's the way of things, sometimes. Ted Owens and I became good friends.

He showed me his files, his toy wagon full of files, and I had some already at home that had been given to me by Puthoff and Targ at SRI International, and as I looked through the many, many documents illustrating instances where he'd produced a wide variety of phenomena, lightning-strikes and weather-changes, heat-waves and cold-waves and hurricane controls and tornado controls and UFO appearances, I found in the files a letter from Dr. Max Fogel, who was the Director of Education for MENSA, the organization of people with high IQ's, and that letter said that Ted Owens had, in 1973, promised Vogel that he would produce a UFO sighting within a certain radius, a 100-mile radius of Norfolk, Virginia, where Owens lived, in that area (he lived actually in Cape Charles, Virginia).

Fogel said, "Yes!" and a UFO appeared that was seen by Policemen, it was reported in the local newspaper in Chase City, Virginia, where the Policemen chased it, and there was an interesting coincidence. The Police Dispatcher who first reported the sighting was a woman named Marian Owen.

It seemed as if -- oftentimes, in these demonstrations -- there would be a person named "Owen" or "Owens" involved! That was another of the Space Intelligences, and it suggested that they had powers outside of our own dimension of Time and Space, that enabled them to create meaningful coincidences.

John Lilly, author of many books, *Center of the Cyclone* was one of his excellent books, *Programming and Meta-programming the Human Biocomputer* -- John Lilly, the great pioneer explorer of Consciousness, often called this kind of a force ECHO, meaning Earth Coincidence Control, some sort of Intelligence that operates outside the normal three dimensions of Space and Time that we experience.

So I asked Ted Owens if he would produce a similar demonstration for me in the San Francisco area where I lived. Could he make a UFO appear like that, and be seen visibly by reliable witnesses. He told me he would do that. He would make a UFO appear in front of many -- hundreds, he said -- of reliable witnesses. It'll be well-attested. It'll be photographed, he said, "You can count on the photograph being published on the front page of one of your local newspapers."

And the story of that demonstration will be presented next, after these messages.

[Segment 3 Follows]

Jeffrey Mishlove: When I got back to San Francisco, I pursued the question with Owens, of his demonstration, and he set it up with me in November of 1976 as follows: he said, "I will cause a UFO to appear. It will happen within 90 days, it will happen within a 100-mile radius of San Francisco." In fact, he said, "I'll cause multiple UFO appearances, and one in particular will be seen by very reliable witnesses. The photograph will be published on the front page of the local newspaper, and that's how you'll know, it'll be my signature."

And other things happened as well. He said, "There will be power blackouts," (that's also one of his signatures).

In December. 1976, it occured pretty much on schedule, December 12th as I recall, in Sonoma State College, a small college campus about 50 miles north of San Francisco. The Art Department, on a clear December day, was sponsoring a live demonstration of an unusual art form -- aerial artwork. A pilot who is an artist was flying his aircraft over the campus, he had smoke trailing out the back of his plane, and he was creating loop-de-loops and other designs in the air.

And this was the demonstration hundreds of students were outside looking up at the sky. Some of them had video-cameras. (This was in the days before camcorders but they were recording it, and there were photographs being taken). Many faculty members were out there.

The pilot of this airplane was named Steve Poleskie, and he was a visiting Professor of Art from Syracuse University. He was visiting Berkeley, and he was performing.

I actually have the videotape of this event.

As he was doing his loop-de-loops about 3,000 feet above the Sonoma State College campus, a UFO appeared right in his airspace. He witnessed it from the air. He said it was about 15-20 feet wide, and it just came out of nowhere. It was right there in his airspace, and it stayed there a few minutes and suddenly disappeared.

It was seen from the ground, and it was photographed. The photograph was published on the front page of one of our local papers, The Berkeley *Gazette*. And the videotape was actually shown on the Channel 9 Evening News, KQED-TV in the San Francisco Bay Area.

Ted Owens had scored pretty much a direct hit.

There were many other events that occurred during that demonstration. There was a UFO Abduction. There was an earthquake, there were power blackouts and other things. So I felt that I now had enough cause to really launch a serious investigation of Ted Owens. I was willing at that point to restructure my graduate program, my doctoral degree program in parapsychology at Berkeley away from the study of Remote Viewing, and make it a case study of Ted Owens!

Little did I know, in my naivete, the kind of opposition that would develop. But I called together a meeting of leading UFO and Parapsychology researchers. I put together a Report, documenting what I had done with Ted Owens, and documenting many other dozens of cases in the records.

And we had J. Allen Hynek attending that meeting, the Founder of The Center for UFO Studies in Evanston, Illinois. We had Dr. James Harder there, who is the Director of Research for the Aerial Phenomenon Research Organization, one of the major UFO organizations at that time.

I had many leading parapsychologists there: D. Scott Rogo, the author of about 20 books on UFO phenomena and parapsychological phenomena attended the meeting. And I thought, with this impressive group of people and this data, that the time had come to launch a serious investigation, to make a major breakthrough in our understanding of the phenomena. And that with these powerful people there, something might be accomplished.

But the tenor of the meeting went in a very different direction. Dr. J. Allen Hynek stood up and said, "I wouldn't touch Ted Owens with a ten-foot pole! That man is exhibiting powers of the subconscious mind, there. They're erratic, they're crazy, they're even dangerous! I don't want to go near him!"

Another/And other researcher said, "He wants to get money from us, that's what this is all about! And furthermore, what if we don't agree with him about certain things. What if we don't comply with all of his wishes? What will he do?"

People were afraid of Ted Owens. And perhaps they had good reason to be afraid of Ted Owens. He was not always the most pleasant of people. He was like an American Folk-Hero, and if you looked at some of his documented demonstrations, many of them of the best ones, in fact, occurred when he would go into a city and announce that he was the "UFO Ambassador" who had come to help people.

And he'd go into a local newspaper and they'd sort of laugh at him, and say, "Come on! Get off of it!" and he'd say, "Oh, you don't believe me. Well, I guess I'll have to teach you a lesson." And sometimes very unpleasant things would happen. I'll go into some of those. But unpleasant weather conditions. Or sometimes even individuals would get ill.

Unpleasant things would happen to particular people who crossed horns with Ted Owens.

This was frightening to some of the researchers whom I had brought together, and the upshot of it all was that in spite of the enormous potential of this phenomenon, from a scientific point of view, nothing came of it.

I was really encouraged to put aside this project and get back to my other studies in Remote Viewing, and indeed I did do that. I wanted to finish my doctoral degree, so I put aside my studies of Ted Owens, at least I was unable to raise funds to do anything serious, and it's unfortunate, because he lived in a relatively impoverished condition in spite of his enormous talents.

But many, many things unfolded from our interactions, and I'll tell you about them after these messages.

[Segment 4 Follows]

Jeffrey Mishlove: Hello, again! I"m Jeffrey Mishlove, host of *Virtual U* on WisdomRadio. I've been talking about my studies and investigations of a most unusual man, Ted Owens, the "PK Man", the "UFO Prophet", the man who taught me how to contact Space Intelligences. A man who was larger than life, somewhat like a Pecos Bill or a Paul Bunyan. I think of him as an American Folk-Hero whose talents had shamanistic qualities, of extraordinary proportions.

One of the researchers to whom I had introduced Ted Owens was D. Scott Rogo. Scott, who is actually a distant cousin of mine -- you see, my mother's maiden name was "Rogo", died in 1990, but this was 1976 and '77. He was the author of more than twenty books dealing with parapsychological phenomena. (By the time of his death, he had authored those books).

Of all the researchers whom I attempted to interest in the Owens case, he became the most interested. In fact, he and I co-authored a book, still unpublished, about the Ted Owens case!

Scott, who was probably in his lifetime, regarded as the single most knowledgeable person about the history of parapsychology and Psychical Research, told me that he thought that Ted Owens might just be the most powerful psychic in all of our history.

He [Rogo] was the author of *Parapsychology: A Century of Inquiry*, one of the best historical books written in the field. We're talking about some great psychics, when you go back to the nineteenth century, people like D. D. Home, or Eursapia Palladino. There are extraordinary things that have been reported in the history of this field, and I will from time to time, talk about them on this program, *Virtual U.*

But Ted Owens was in a class of his own, really. We're talking about earthquake control, hurricane control, volcanoes, tornadoes, the forces of Nature seemed to respond to his thoughts.

One of my friends, the Jungian scholar, Dr. James Driscoll, felt that Owens was in touch with the archetypal energies of the Greek god Poseidon, the god of the sea. The god whose thoughts were expressed in the elemental forces of Earth, Air, Fire, and Water.

Owens himself saw it a little differently. If we look at his life history, he knew from childhood that he had some unusual experiences. When he went into the Military in World War II, he was in the Navy, and he describes for example, both in his childhood and again in the Navy, there were moments, like diving from the air from a diving-board into a swimming-pool, that he felt like he was suspended in mid-air for a while, and that people down below would see this, and marvel at it!

So while he was in the Navy and producing effects like this, from time to time, and having other experiences, he wrote to J. B. Rhine, who was at Duke University, who had established a Parapsychology Laboratory there, and would you believe it, J. B. Rhine invited Owens to come to Duke University and work for him as a Laboratory Assistant.

Rhine took an interest in Owens and his talents! And Owens did. He enrolled as an undergraduate student at Duke University, and he worked for J. B. Rhine, and he became very close to J. B. and his wife Louisa Rhine. At that time he learned about the scientific research that was being undertaken at Duke University in the field of extrasensory perception.

J. B. Rhine had established an international reputation for his work in card-guessing and for his work in psychokinesis, where he'd ask people to concentrate on dice: he had a machine that would throw dice, and ask people to make certain faces of these dice come face-up.

Owens, of course, was working in a wilder way, in a less disciplined way with these phenomena. He told me on one occasion, he was in the office, in the laboratory with Rhine and some of the research associates, and there was a scissors on the table, and he concentrated on that scissors, and it levitated a few feet above the table! I tried to verify that event by talking to Dr. Rhine and his wife.

Of course many decades later, nobody remembered it. But you know? They didn't really want to talk about Ted Owens either. I think they considered him an embarrassment. The Rhines had really, really struggled to make Parapsychology a respectable scientific discipline, and it was an uphill struggle because the Scientific Community wasn't ready to accept even statistical experimental, well-controlled proof of such a thing as extrasensory perception, and in psychokinesis, let alone to think of someone of the likes of Ted Owens!

It took until the mid-1960's, in fact 1969, before the American Association for the Advancement of Science granted recognition to the Parapsychological Association as an affiliate body, to even recognize that they were doing valid Science! And that was roughly about 40 years from the time that J. B. Rhine first initiated his research.

So his struggles just put Parapsychology on the map, [but] prevented him from really appreciating not just Ted Owens, but many of the more far-out, more extraordinary, bizarre, remarkable, strange phenomena in the parapsychological zoo, so to speak! But Ted Owens did get his training right there, with the "Father of Parapsychology", J. B. Rhine.

He got married when he was an undergraduate student, and left Duke University, and it was after that, that he really began focusing his energies on controlling the weather. He thought that he was in touch with the Powers of Nature when he observed that he could concentrate and cause clouds to move about, or cause lightning to strike, or cause storms to appear.

I'll tell you more about his remarkable story, after these messages.

[Segment 4-Coda Follows]

Jeffrey Mishlove: Welcome back to *Virtual U.* I'm your host, Jeffrey Mishlove, and I've been talking about my encounters with a man who taught me how to contact Space Intelligences. It's really quite a dramatic tale, and one that I rarely tell, because it is so bizarre. But there are many deep insights that I've gleaned from this story, and I'll be back at 6 and a half minutes after the hour, for another hour, in which I'll go into much more depth about not only the phenomena which I observed, but the metaphysical lessons associated with that.

....

Before we end this hour, I should say some things about Ted Owens. He was a bizarre person. One might say that he had strange personality quirks, that he was even frightening and unpredictable and unpleasant and egotistical, and sometimes paranoid, and perhaps even psychotic. But he had an extraordinary gift, not only the gift of producing miraculous phenomena, but there was a core to him that was very pure.

A core to him that was in touch with an extraordinarily powerful spiritual essence. I want to let you know that because I'll be talking about that more when I return from our break ....

[Segment 5 Follows]

Jeffrey Mishlove: Welcome back to *Virtual U.* I'm your host, Jeffrey Mishlove, and this is our second hour of exploring the phenomenon of Space Intelligences. Well, I haven't really gotten into Space Intelligences too much yet! What I've actually been talking about is my encounter with the "Ambassador of the Space Intelligences", Ted Owens, a man I studied from 1976, when I first met him, until his death in 1987.

During that eleven-year period, he produced about 200 documented demonstrations of unusual phenomena, which he attributed to the Space Intelligences with which he claimed to be in telepathic contact.

Let me say a few more things about Ted. We were describing, before the break, how he had studied at Duke University in the 1940's -- around 1947. He actually was Research Assistant to Professor J. B. Rhine in the Parapsychology Laboratory there. He had left Duke University with his wife, travelling around the country, working at various odd jobs.

Notice that he seemed to have an ability to control the weather with his thoughts! If he wanted to make a storm come up, he'd think about it, he'd visualize a storm and it would happen. This seemed to happen over and over again. It got to the point where at one time, he even contacted the C.I.A. and offered to demonstrate it to them. In fact, throughout his career, he made a real effort to interest the United States Government in working with what he believed were his unusual powers.

I think the United States Government probably has extensive files on him, because he was constantly bombarding them with information. But they were really ill-equipped to deal with a person like him, and as far as I can tell, while they kept files on him, and maybe had people watching him from time to time, nothing ever came of those contacts.

At some point, Ted shifted in his viewpoint. He originally thought it was "Nature": he was in touch with Nature. And because it was his link with Nature itself, he was able to produce these phenomena. And on one occasion, he actually saw a UFO while he was producing the phenomenon.

There was a big UFO flap across the United States, back in the 1960's and it dawned on him then that it wasn't just "Nature", that he was in touch with some phenomenon in space and time as we normally think of it, the phenomenon he began to the S.I.'s or the Space Intelligences.

He began to receive what he described as telepathic messages from the Space Intelligences. You might think that he had gone totally off his rocker at this point, but he believed that he had had a whole series of unusual experiences that made him believe that he had been abducted and had actually had surgery performed on his brain, that enhanced his natural telepathic abilities and allowed this to occur.

Truly, as a psychotherapist, I can tell you that these kinds of stories are indicative of paranoid psychosis or schizophrenic psychosis. These are the stories of a schizophrenic, of a psychotic person, of an insane person, of a crazy person. It's no surprise to me that people treated Ted Owens this way.

I think perhaps what is unusual about me is that I was willing to say, "All right, Mister, what is your evidence?" And if you listened to the first hour of this program, you know already that Ted Owens produced a great deal of evidence for me. In fact, I have in my files, hundreds of cases of weather-control and UFO appearances and poltergeist types of phenomena that were associated with his demonstrations. Typically, what he would do to produce a demonstration is put in writing, to scientists or journalists, or other responsible members of Society, what he planned to do, usually something very unusual or bizarre -- a heat wave, a cold wave, a UFO appearance, and then he would forward newspaper clippings of these events, because they were so dramatic, they were reported in the newspapers.

I have these in my files along with the original envelopes and postmarks and letters documenting the precise dates in which his predictions were made. He'd send them to multiple groups of scientists to make sure they were well documented, and many of these scientists, who really wanted little to do with Ted Owens, were happy to forward to me all of their documentation about the man.

Well, he came to see himself as the agent of the Space Intelligences as their representative on Earth. Then he began to tell me as I questioned him about the course of his life, he began to tell me some very interesting things.

He told me, for example, that he believed that the Space Intelligences had been watching him throughout the course of his life, and he pointed out to me that he had held many different occupations. He had been a knife-thrower in a circus act and a bullwhip artist in a circus act. And he had been a high-speed typist, and he had been a jazz musician, a drummer. He had worked at a railroad as what he called an "idea man".

He had been in the Navy. He had been a Parapsychology Assistant to J. B. Rhine at Duke University. He had worked in a law office. Owens believed that all of these strange careers were somehow guided or arranged for him by the Space Intelligences, and they had a purpose.

The purpose was to help him develop a Mind that was so flexible that it was capable of developing very complex symbols from many different occupations, and professions, so that he could use those symbols in his telepathic contact with them.

He also told me that these Space Intelligences had tried throughout history to try to establish such contact with many human beings from time to time. He said Moses was such a person. And often he compared himself to Moses.

I think when one considers the accounts of Moses, in the *Book of Exodus*, and the miracles that were produced in Egypt at that time, ostensibly (I have no idea whether any of that really happened -- there's no archeological or other evidence to support that any of that story is true; I consider it very likely a story of mythological dimensions more than actual, but people will differ on these things) and in any case one can see the parallels.

Owens, with his abilities to end droughts, with his abilities to cause UFO appearances and many, many other things, seemed to have powers parallel to those of Moses.

On one occasion, parapsychologist D. Scott Rogo and I observed for a month or more, Owens's ability to manipulate the movements of a hurricane in the Caribbean, off the coast of Florida. Day by day, he was doing this. One direction, then another direction, and reporting to us in advance what was going on, all of this is well documented. And today there are still hundreds of people who have witnessed these demonstrations of Ted Owens.

I have been in touch with many of them, and I have their affidavits on record. For example -- and this is a Moses-like phenomenon -- I have the affidavit of Attorney Sidney Margulies in the Philadelphia area, who was working in a law office where Ted Owens was employed, back in the late 1960's (about 1967), when Owens was bragging to him, as they were standing in the stairwell of this office building, that he could control the weather.

Margulies said to him, "Well, if you're so good, why don't you make lightning strike right there," the Camden Bridge, and Owen pointed his finger. (It was a cloudy day but not lightning), and within a minute a bolt of lightning came out of the sky -- the only bolt of lightning in the sky at that time, and struck that Bridge, right where Owens was pointing.

And that Attorney, Sidney Margulies, wrote an affidavit attesting to his witnessing that fact, and I have spoken to him. I have other Affidavits of exactly that phenomenon -- Owens's ability to point his finger and concentrate, and cause lightning to strike. That's an unusual phenomenon, and we know scientifically speaking, that the odds of predicting when lightning is going to strike are less than one in a million.

That event alone is highly significant for me, from a scientific point of view.

Owens tried, throughout his career, to encourage the United States Government to work with him. He felt that our world was in great danger, that we were on the brink of a nuclear war. Back then, in the sixties and seventies, many, many intelligent people were in agreement about the dangers that the world was in. I think that these days, it seems like somewhat of a less dangerous place than it did, back then, because of the Cold War and hostilities between the communist world and the capitalist world, that were going on at that time.

He believed that his intervention, or the intervention of the UFO's, was required, literally, to save the world. But he was laughed at, and when he was laughed at, as I mentioned before, he sometimes produced demonstrations that were unpleasant in nature.

In one instance, he came to San Francisco in the summer of '77 and he announced that he was here to end the drought. We were having another drought then, and he walked into the offices of the San Francisco *Examiner* and *Chronicle*, in order to make his public proclamation that he, the UFO Prophet, had come to end the drought.

The guard in the lobby literally kicked him right out the door! So he said he would have to teach the people of California a lesson, and instead of ending the drought, he would cause forest fires. He said forest fires would be caused by lightning, his trademark.

I was a witness to this. Within weeks, 300,000 acres in California had burned. A thousand fires had been started by lightning. It was one of the worst devastations. It affected not only California but the Western States as well. I was horrified, I was aghast. I guess I have/had a little more distance from the phenomenon then.

I went to the *Examiner* myself, to report what I had documented, because Owens had sent me in writing his prediction that he would cause these fires and then they had occurred. I met with a reporter who was a close friend of an associate of mine. We met at a restaurant for dinner and I began to explain to him the whole sequence of events and he got so indignant that I was telling him this preposterous tale, that he got up and walked out of the dinner-table, and I have never seen that reporter, whose name was Sandy Zane, since that time, well over twenty years ago!

That was the problem, of getting people to take this phenomenon seriously. I'll be back again after these messages.

How To Contact The Space People

[Break]

Jeffrey Mishlove: Hello again, I'm Jeffrey Mishlove, host of *Virtual U*, and I've been talking about my eleven-year research with the UFO Prophet, the "PK Man", Ted Owens.

I guess I've been tantalizing you, the audience members, by telling you that what this program is about is contacting Space Intelligences. Ted Owens wrote the book, *How to Contact Space People*. It was published by Saucerian Press in 1969 in Clarksburg, West Virginia.

That book is a rare, out-of-print classic now, and for the rest of this program, I'm about to talk about that process of contacting Space Intelligences. I'm really giving you a lot of background about Ted Owens because I think it's important that people understand the range and the depth of the phenomena that we're discussing. It's the kind of phenomena that might be called, in the classic Greek sense, daimonic.

You might think, from the Christian theological perspective, it's demonic, and many Christian theologians think that UFO phenomena are the work of the devil! But in the Greek sense of the term, a daimon was a spirit that had both positive and negative qualities.

That seems to be more an appropriate way to classify the Owens phenomena, and the Space Intelligences with which he worked. He had a training program, himself. He had students. I interviewed a number of these students.

One was named Jade Swan, and she had a cousin or sister-in-law named Janice Leslie. I've lost touch with both of these women, and I'm mentioning their names now because it's been well over a decade since I interviewed either of them, but perhaps they'll hear this program, or somebody who knows them will hear this program and urge them to get in touch with me, through WisdomRadio or through the *Virtual U* program or through my website, www.mishlove.com. (That's my name).

They took his program and they were interested in using it the way he used it. They were interested in going out into the woods late at night and making lights appear in the sky. They described the many different kinds of lights. There were some that would zip across the sky. and they called them the zippers.

Then there were other lights that would hover, right above the tree-tops, and they went on many adventures like this, after being trained by Ted Owens to do this kind of work. I also took the Ted Owens Training Program, and I'm going to describe it as we move on through the hour here.

I've also interviewed other people who have as well. Ted Owens told people that this kind of a contact with an other-dimensional Intelligence could be used in many different ways. If you had his makeup, his personality, his stamina, you might want to go out and cause UFO sightings or poltergeist types of appearances.

But other people use the same kind of training purpose for healing. When Ted Owens asked me, when I finally took his training in January of 1986, about a year before his death, he asked me, "Jeffrey, what would you like to do? What is your purpose? What is your intention in going through this Training Program to contact Space Intelligences?"

And I thought about it. I said, "Ted, what I really want to do with my life is to become an effective communicator to the public at large about the realities of the Spirit, about the realities of Parapsychology and Consciousness."

I was at a low point in my life, because even though I had a doctoral degree in Parapsychology, even though I'd been on the radio, going back to the 1970's, I had been slandered and libeled. Because after I received my doctoral degree, I had become a target for the skeptics. It was intolerable to them that a person like me, a public figure, would have the visibility and the public credibility to talk about the kinds of phenomena that I was researching and experiencing, and they had launched a big effort to actually get the University of California to revoke my doctoral degree in Parapsychology.

Which, incidentally, is the only doctoral degree in Parapsychology ever awarded by an accredited American University. It was a landmark of sorts, and it remains so today, twenty years later.

When they were unsuccessful in getting that degree revoked, an article about me was published, arranged by the skeptics, it was published in Psychology Today, which then had a circulation of nearly a million readers, claiming that I probably really didn't get the degree, and if I did get it, I certainly didn't deserve it because I was nothing but a bad person, all the way around. And I felt mortified, and I withdrew from the field, and I did other things.

I got my training in psychotherapy. I got business experience. I studied computers and computer programming. Anything but being in public in the fields that I loved. Of consciousness, of spirituality, of parapsychology.

But I asked Ted Owens then for that gift, that I be out there in the world, that I could be an effective communicator once again, for the realities that I knew so deeply.

I can tell you this. Within a few months of taking that training, I launched my *Thinking Allowed* television series. 1986. It was launched in May.

We have now been producing programs every week since then, continuously, and we've been out on the Satellite all over North America every week since then. The TV program is carried by Wisdom Television, and it's carried by Public Television Stations throughout the United States and Canada.

So I got my wish. And I have to say, that connection with the Space Intelligences was very positive and wholesome for me. And now, dear listeners, if you could contact Space Intelligences with such powers, what would you wish for?

What would be your mission, your purpose? What would you like to fulfill?

I"ll be back.

[Break]

Jeffrey Mishlove: Welcome back to *Virtual U.* I'm your host, Jeffrey Mishlove. And I've been talking today about contacting Space Intelligences. My experience in this realm is multifold. It has to do with eleven years of personal relationship in a research project with the UFO Prophet and PK Man, Ted Owens, an individual who died in relative obscurity in 1987, but during the time that I knew him, he produced hundreds of what would have to be called "miraculous events".

Healings, weather-control demonstrations, demonstrations of UFO appearances, training other people to produce such unusual phenomena.

During that time I also had a long-standing interest in UFO's. I had a long-standing interest in Parapsychology, and a long-standing interest in Spirituality, Mysticism, and Consciousness, and a long-standing interest in an important question relating to Space Intelligences, and that is, the mathematics of higher dimensions of space.

We talk about the Spirit Worlds. We talk about aliens coming from other dimensions of Space and Time. We have dream worlds. We have the worlds of Shamanism. We have the worlds of Mythology, the worlds of the gods and the goddesses, and many, many other mythological creatures.

I postulate that if there is any reality at all to these ideas of other worlds -- of spirit worlds, and dream worlds, and a life after death -- if these things exist, they have to exist somewhere. Since they apparently don't exist in the three-dimensional space that we observe through our normal senses, perhaps there is another space where they exist.

Perhaps other dimensions of space beside the three dimensions that we normally experience with our senses, and indeed, mathematicians have for a long time known that it's no problem to mathematically postulate other dimensions of space.

For probably over a century now, mathematicians have asked questions like this: If there were four dimensions of space or five dimensions of space, what would it be like geometrically, topologically? If you had a sphere, and you wanted to pile up a bunch of spheres, how would they pile up, in higher dimensions of space?

You know, you can take a quarter and set it down on a table, and you can pack six quarters, and they all fit around the one quarter. That's on one dimension, a single plane -- actually, two dimensions. A plane is two dimensions.

In three dimensions you can take a sphere and pack other spheres around a sphere, like a pile of cannonballs.

In higher dimensions of space, each time you get more and more of these higher-dimensional objects you can pack against each other. So mathematicians have studied this for a long time. There are even people who've been gifted with the ability to visualize what higher dimensions of space are like! They've been studied by mathematicians.

But now we live in an era in which physics itself -- :"Mainstream Physics" -- considers higher dimensions of Physics to be not only routine but even necessary. Probably today the leading theory in mainstream physics is known as superstring theory, and it is the theory that unifies Einstein's relativity. His General Relativity. His theory of cosmology, that deals with the force of gravity. That deals with the size and age of the universe as a whole, the physical universe as we know it.

With quantum theory. Quantum theory is a very powerful Theory developed in the earlier part of the Twentieth Century that accounts for all of the properties of subatomic particles. So when you can unify general relativity with quantum theory, you're unifying the very, very large with the very, very small.

Physicists today are hopeful that superstring theory will be something akin to a "final Theory", a theory of everything that is known in physics.

The unusual thing about superstring theory -- it seems to be working quite well, there are now thousands of physicists engaged in the project of building and refining all of the nuances of superstring theory. But that is a theory that does indeed entail higher dimensions of space, to be precise 9 dimensions of space, one dimension of time, so it's a ten-dimensional theory.

When you get into more of the fine points of superstring theory, you see that the 10 dimensions unfold into maybe 24 and 36 and up and up and up to virtually infinite numbers of dimensions in space!

The thought is, that the universe first expanded, at the moment of creation, from the big bang, that the three dimensions that we experience with our senses, expanded, but the other 9 dimensions of space remained as small as they were at the time of the big bang, a kind of infinitesimally small point of Space.

So we don't experience those dimensions. Our bodies, you might say, are too big, but they're there in/And our minds, perhaps, do experience those dimensions. Perhaps we experience them in dreaming. Perhaps after we die, after we separate from our bodies, perhaps we can exist in those dimensions, because even though they're tiny, tiny, infinitesimally tiny, size may not matter.

We might exist and be no larger than a subatomic particle or a quark ourselves, moving and vibrating through these 10 dimensions and other dimensions. Size may have a totally different meaning for us.

So what I think about these "higher dimensions of space", I have a mathematical, scientific appreciation for the fact that they're not absurd, and that they very well may relate to what we may think of as alien encounters and mythological encounters, and life after death, and dreams.

I'll be back with more after these messages.

[Segment 8 Follows]

Jeffrey Mishlove: Welcome back to *Virtual U*, I'm Jeffrey Mishlove. We've been talking about Space Intelligence[s], and now I'd like to share with you one of the exercises for contacting Space Intelligences that was taught to me by Ted Owens.

I'd like you to begin by thinking for yourself what you really want most for your life. What would be the most meaningful, the most rewarding experience that you could have, an experience that would fulfill your soul?

Think of that. And also think about what you would like to contribute to this world. And hold those thoughts in your mind.

Let me ask you now to close your eyes, if you would, if you feel comfortable doing that. And visualize yourself moving through space, travelling to a very distant part of the universe, beyond out solar system, beyond our galaxy. Beyond the cluster of galaxies of which our Milky Way galaxy is a part.

Moving out farther and farther into the very depths of the Universe itself. As you get farther and farther, you'll notice that there is a massive superstructure, the great attractor, the great wall of galaxies -- a huge structure, as if the galaxies themselves are the membranes of a giant cell, and that the universe is a living organism.

We can move even further, so that our local cell in the universe becomes smaller and smaller and fades away, and we're experiencing the wholeness and the wonder and the radiance of the universe as a whole, coming to a place of great beauty.

A place where the sky is turquoise-blue and there are pink clouds and yellow clouds in the sky, a place of great comfort and pleasantness.

And imagine if you will, a glass sphere. A crystalline clear sphere suspended in this brilliant blue and pink sky. And allow yourself as you float through space, floating through the universe, to just enter into that sphere in your imagination.

Entering into that sphere, you shed the gross part of your nature, and you become like a spirit being yourself, freed -- although you're not even in a physical body -- but freed from any heaviness, freed from a sense of emotional attachment, the pure essence within you, there in that sphere.

And there you'll find a place where you can settle -- a chair, a place where you can sit. And you'll see a similar place across from you, and a being is there, a being of great beauty and wisdom. Perhaps an older man or an older woman or an androgynous being. An ancient being.

And as you look at the face of that ancient being, you see many things. You may be frightened but above all you feel great peace, and bliss and knowledge, letting go of fear. And just communing with that being, that being from beyond space and time as we think of it.

Not a word is said, but knowledge and wisdom is shared. You feel a sense growing within you of connection with your life's purpose. A connection with your destiny. A connection with the inner resources that will enable you to function in a way that is more in tune with your own deepest nature, more in tune with your own spiritual essence, more in tune with God, in the finest way that you understand God to be.

More in tune with nature. More in tune with the life force within you. Harmonizing your vibrations, resynchronizing your energies. Clarifying your thoughts and your vision.

And allow yourself to enjoy this communion, to enjoy this connection, to feel it flowing within your being [pause] knowing that even as you experience this crystalline place, and the farther reaches of the universe, you're also listening to WisdomRadio! In a body on Planet Earth.

And now gradually, gently, allowing yourself to return to that body, bringing with you all the memories of that encounter, bringing with you the knowledge of the communion that you experienced, bringing with you the sense connection, knowing that you can re-establish this contact with this great, wise, ancient one.

Opening your eyes, returning to your room, looking about, knowing that you're listening to *Virtual U* on WisdomRadio.

And I am your host, Jeffrey Mishlove, it's been a pleasure sharing this two-hour program with you, exploring Space Intelligence. Exploring, really, human potential and its possibilities! And I shall return again after these messages.

[Below is Segment 8-Coda to the end of this Program]

Jeffrey Mishlove: The music that you're listening to for *Virtual U* was composed by Gary Takesian, and produced for *Virtual U* by Lars Spivock. ....

We've had two hours together exploring the many dimensions and wonders of contact with Space Intelligence, from the spiritual to the shamanistic to the UFO dimensions and the life of Ted Owens, something like a Pecos Bill or a Paul Bunyan -- a larger-than-life folk character who I had the great privilege for eleven years before his death in 1987.

Thank you so much for being with me in this Program, allowing me to share one of the deepest nuggets of gold of my life. I wish you well. Goodnight.

BOOK ONE :

HOW TO CONTACT SPACE PEOPLE

Ted Owens

CHAPTER ONE
MY EARLY EXPERIMENTS

During the last three years I have successfully communicated with UFO's ... flying saucers ... which, henceforth, I will call SI's (Saucer Intelligences). My absolute, undisputable proof of this lies in the fact that, prior to UFO, or SI, appearances and actions, I would write to various government agencies, scientists, and responsible people, and state that the SI's would appear, and/or when, and at times what they would do. Then, after it occurred and was written up in the newspapers, I would append the news clips to my letter, written some days or weeks before, and have a complete case of successful, proved communication with the SI's. In this book you will see signed, notarized statements from responsible people to the effect that I have done this. And in this book I will tell you, the reader, the secret of my communication with the saucer intelligences so that you, too, can try your hand at communicating with these remarkable, more-powerful-than-we, UFO Intelligences. Before we get into that, let me put some of my concrete proof in front of you, the reader, so that you can realize an almost unbelievable statement: that I am the only human being alive able to communicate, TWO WAYS, with the SI's, and prove it.

Following are the names and addresses of government agencies, scientists, and responsible persons to whom I have been sending predictions on UFO appearances and actions these past few years. These government agencies and scientists are, quite naturally, bashful about giving me signed, notarized statements, because they feel they might be help up to ridicule. However, if they so wished, they could do so, for they have received the very same predictions and information that the responsible persons received, and who did in fact give me said signed, notarized statements, knowing that it was a miraculous fact, and not being afraid to say so.

Pat Shannon, a Notary Public of the State of California,
living at 26005 Oak Street, #18, Lomita, California.

Zelda Hansel, wife of an electronics expert,
29 S. Wyoming, Ardmore, Pa.

Roland Swank, scientist, Organization of Scientific Research,
Box 562, Paoli, Pa.

Mrs. Louise Rhine, scientist,
P.O. Box 46, Rt. 3, Hillsboro, N.C.

Jack McKinney, "Night Talk Show", WCAU,
4100 City Line Avenue, Philadelphia, Pa.

George Clark, Central Intelligence Agency, Washington, D.C.

Mr. Eastwood, Inventions, N.A.S.A., Washington, D.C.

It might well mentioned here that I have a "code name" in my correspondence with CIA and NASA that of "P K Man". I should also like to mention that, although I have been demonstrating literal miracles for these two government agencies, I am not employed with them, nor have I any connection with them, other than corresponding with them.

Exhibit "A" is a signed, notarized statement from Patricia Shannon.

Exhibit "B" is a signed, notarized statement from Zelda Hansell.

(Note: The above two parties do not know each other. They are complete strangers, as are most of the other agencies and parties who have received my predictions ahead of the events which were to happen. Also keep in mind that, although these are called "predictions", what actually happened was that I wrote the "predictions", then communicated with SI's and asked them to appear, as a signal of confirmation that we were in fact in communication with each other.)

Exhibit "C" is Mrs. Mangels, of Washington D.C., for whom I produced an earthquake by communicating with the SI's and asking for one, specifically on the West Coast.

Exhibit "D" is a signed, notarized statement from a top lawyer, who stood beside me and watched me produce a bolt of lightning where he pointed, after I communicated with the SI's and asked for it.

Exhibit "E" is a sample of one of my many successful "predictions" to Roland Swank, scientist. This particular one deals with the now-famous Hurricane Inez, which struck in 1966. I was busily demonstrating to the scientists how the SI's would actually control and guide this hurricane completely counter to the predictions of the U.S. Weather Bureau and Miami Hurricane Center. Inez, as you perhaps know, was not supposed to turn at Cuba and approach the U.S. But I asked the SI's to make it do so, and it turned sharply and went to Miami. Then it was supposed to go up the East Coast, so I asked the SI's to stop it, and back it up and take Hurricane Betsy's old track. Swank told me personally that each time I would tell the scientists I would change the hurricane's course, they would laugh heartily - until the cane followed my course, and not that of the Miami Hurricane Center. And when it stopped and backed up, as per my ahead-prediction, he said the scientists were shocked and electrified.

These are just a few of the 180 cases I have, fully documented, of my communication with the SI's. Later I plan to do a large, comprehensive book, detailing each and every one of these cases, which are literal miracles. But for now, the reader is interested only in how to talk with the UFO's, and so we shall proceed along these lines.

****

In order for the reader to understand that I am just like himself, or herself - that is, not a scientist or professional man such as a lawyer or doctor - so that it must be possible for him or her to apply the same techniques that I have used in order to talk with flying saucers, it is necessary for me to present, as briefly as possible, a record of my activity which led me to this discovery of talking with UFO's.

While living at Ft. Worth, Texas, in the late 1960's, my daughter and I were out driving in the country one night, when a cigar-shaped UFO suddenly appeared at our left, over a field, and came floating toward our car, making no noise, with red, white, blue, and green colors flaming vividly from it. Its nose was tilted down towards the ground. As we watched; it approached close to our car, then instantly vanished, just like a light turned off.

From that day on, my life changed radically. I was working in the field of hypnotism (specializing in teaching auto-hypnosis to people from all walks of life). Ideas began to flood in on me, pertaining to the healing of persons who were sick and unhappy, until these ideas filled a large book. I applied many of the ideas, and saved many persons who could not be helped by orthodox means. Then the local medical fraternity accused me of "practicing medicine without a license" and we had to leave Ft. Worth.

While in Ft. Worth I gave my daughter, Lornie, several demonstrations of making lightning strike in certain areas during thundershowers. I was playfully experimenting with a theory I had on the practical application of "PK" or psychokinetic power to nature's forces. Some time later our family moved to Phoenix, Arizona, which was in the midst of a terrible drought. The idea to experiment with ESP for weather control came to me again, so I gathered my children together and showed them how I would make it storm. It did, so intensely that the city was declared a disaster area. To make sure that it was I who had brought this about, and not just a coincidence, I announced to my family we would make a series of storms - and I wrote in to the local papers to that effect. I produced eight terrible, rocking thunderstorms complete with tremendous lightning displays, within a period of three weeks.

During one storm I was out in the yard waving my hand (I am going to tell you how to do this, later in this book) lightning struck our house twice, and all the neighbors ran over to our house to see if it was on fire, or if we were hurt.

Electrified by my success, and knowing for certain that I had something, I wrote to government agencies and many important people, but to no avail. No one would believe me. We moved then to Los Angeles, also in the middle of a drought, and I made some tremendous storms there. On our way we drove through Las Vegas, and I made a terrible storm there, just to keep in practice. It nearly wrecked the town. We went clear across a breather. Now, I figured that somehow I had managed to contact the essence of the intelligence behind nature herself. And while resting in Myrtle Beach, an idea occurred to me. A hurricane had appeared, off Florida, so I called my kids together, drew a map and a course for the hurricane to follow (using southern Florida as a bullseye) else no one would believe me later on, and wrote to government agencies and scientists about what I was doing. To the amazement of our family, the hurricane (Cleo) followed my map to the letter! If it would start to deviate from its target, I would communicate with "Nature" and get it back onto the course I had prescribed. During that season I successfully directed three hurricanes to our improvised target!

Then we went to Washington, and I talked with George Clark of the CIA. First, I told him who I was, and what I had been doing, and that I had been writing his agency ahead of events which had actually happened. I told him I wouldn't blame him if he unceremoniously threw me out of the CIA offices, because it seemed so fantastic. No, he said, he was interested - and he talked with the children and myself for an hour or two about it. However I got not action on it.

We went to N.A.S.A. and talked with a Mr. Eastwood, of Inventions. He also was fascinated, and we spent an hour or two with him, explaining the whole thing. But again, no action.

Ted Owens

CHAPTER TWO
THE UFO INTELLIGENCES

Having made no headway with the U.S. Government, I had to get a job, and a house for my family. Our car had just fallen apart after our long, long trip across the U.S., and I was near broke.

It was precisely at this point that I discovered for the first time that it was not nature, but the UFO INTELLIGENCES, which I had been contacting, and which had been guiding me.

We had just settled into our rented house in Washington, D.C., and I had gotten a job, when UFO's starting appearing all around the area. The newspapers and TV were full of reports. Still, I had not connected what I was doing with UFO's. But one day the "intelligence from Nature" told me to write a letter to George Clark of Central Intelligence.

My letter read:

> Nature has told me to tell you that to prove it is using me as its representative, it will do something without my using PK, or knowing any of its (Nature's) workings. Nature will in the near future, change the North and South poles. As the message came to me, I believe it will use extreme heat to affect those two places, and change the magnetic condition of the Poles. Nature added that you won't have to check with any Bureau on it - that the results will be strong enough to make the newspapers, where you can read about it.

(I actually delayed sending this letter to him, because, as I told my children, the Intelligence didn't seem to make any sense. But, since Nature's other messages had mostly all come to pass, I finally went ahead, after days of vacillation, and sent the letter.)

It was dated March 9, 1965. On July 8 of that year I found out, with a jolt, that what I had been dealing with for several years were UFO Intelligences. On July 8, all the newspapers carried a startling article:

> FLYING SAUCER IS REPORTED OVER TWO SOUTH POLES.
>
> AP, Santiago, Chile.
>
> From the Antarctic Thursday came official reports that a mysterious lens-shaped flying object, maneuvering and moving at great speed, was sighted last Saturday. A Chilean base commander in the Antarctic reported the object was "yellowish red, changing to green, yellow and orange".
>
> In Buenos Aires, the Navy issued a communique saying personnel at Argentina's Antarctic base saw the flying object and photographed it. Mario J. Berrero, commander of the Chilean base, told the Defense Ministry by radio that it would be too much to say that all of us saw a flying saucer, one of those science-fiction things. However," he continued, "it was something real, an object that moved at amazing speed, maneuvered quickly, and gave off a blue-green sheen. It also caused interference in the electromagnetic apparatus of an Argentine base which is facing ours on a nearby small island." The interference was confirmed by the Navy communique issued in Buenos Aires. "The object was yellowish red," Berrero said, "changing to green, yellow and orange. It would zigzag quickly. Then it stopped and we promptly reached for field glasses, telescopes, anything at hand to sight it. We watched as it remained quietly there for about 20 minutes."

> Berrero said a corporal took color pictures but there are no facilities for developing the film. The men must wait for eight months to be relieved to have the film developed on the mainland.

So, my prediction "from Nature", to George Clark, months earlier, had come to pass. There had been an electromagnetic change over the Pole; and the flying saucer had calmly stayed in place over the scientific base long enough to be photographed, and to get into the newspapers. Thus, ingeniously, the UFO intelligences had made my "prediction" come true, and had told me that it was they, and not Nature, who had been communicating with me. Moreover, as per my letter, they confirmed by this action that they were in communication with me.

Still the government did nothing. My two teen-agers, Lornie and Rick, who had been with me through several years of SI-caused miracles, went to the West Coast to live with their mother, and to prepare for college. My wife and I and my small baby went to Philadelphia to live. Then the fun really started.

At this point you, the reader, might like to guess who, besides the U.S. Government had knowledge of my causing storms and guiding hurricanes, through the SI's. Give up? RUSSIA!

On October 1. 1964, the following clipping appeared in the newspapers:

> U.S. SAID WAGING WEATHER WAR. Moscow, Sept. 30, AP.
>
> A Soviet colonel charged in Moscow Wednesday that the Pentagon had directed US scientists to work out ways of directing hurricanes toward Communist countries (Meaning Cuba). The charge was made by Col. I. Zheitikov in the Soviet Defense Ministry newspaper Krasnaya Zvezda (Red Star).

I almost fell off my chair laughing, when I read that, because I had actually guided three hurricanes onto Florida, as a demonstration for the U.S. Government; and of course Cuba had been affected, infuriating Russia. What startled me was the fact that Russia, knowing nothing about my activity, had perceived that all those hurricanes crisscrossing Cuba, toward the U.S., could not be accidents, or coincidences! Of course, if the Russians had stopped to think, if the U.S. could direct hurricanes (it cannot) it would not deliberately steer three of the giants onto its own country, Florida!

On July 21, 1965, I again wrote George Clark, CIA, as follows:

> Dear George:
>
> (1) My little friends say that they will appear over one of our major U.S. cities soon, in one of their flying machines. They won't name the city, for security reasons (theirs).
>
> (2) They also state that they will begin an attack campaign on the U.S. with lightning. Lightning attacks everywhere. There will be an unusual abundance of lightning bolts striking everywhere, everything, soon.
>
> The above is an effort to further prove that PK Man (Owens) is their representative, and that they can communicate with PK Man.

The SI's went to work immediately. News clips, as usual, tell the story. July 23, two days later came the headline,

> LIGHTNING KILLS POULTRY WORKER IN HOME CELLAR.
>
> Oceanville, New Jersey:
>
> A lightning bolt struck a man who was counting chicken eggs 10 feet beneath the earth, in a cellar. He had just picked up a telephone to call his family to warn that lightning had just struck a tree outside the cellar. Then it struck again, through the telephone connection.

July 30: Three U.S. Marines were struck and killed by a bolt of lightning in Viet Nam.

Aug. 4: Lightning struck a Saturn 5 Moon Rocket launch pad at Cape Kennedy, killing one man and injuring five.

Aug. 9: Two golfers were struck and killed by a bolt of lightning in Louisville, Georgia.

Aug. 17: In Auburn, Calif., a bolt of lightning struck and exploded a stockpile of dynamite at Hell Hole Dam, killing three men and injuring a fourth.

Aug. 19: In Porterville, California, a bolt of lighting struck and set on fire one of the oldest and largest living things on earth - Old Solo, a giant, 202-foot-high redwood tree.

Aug. 19: A line of thunderstorms moved through Philadelphia, Pa., with lightning bolts striking everywhere. Thousands of homes and businesses were blacked out.

Aug. 20: Over Saint-Trond, Belgium, a Polish airliner was struck by a bolt of lightning and exploded.

(Note: All of the above examples were carried widely in the newspapers.)

Now, for the other parts of the prediction, that the SI's would make an appearance over a U.S. city.

> July 31: Washington, D.C.
>
> People on five continents have reported gazing into the sky in recent weeks, usually at night, and seeing something they couldn't explain. Suddenly, the flying saucer phenomena is back with us. From the United States, from Argentina, Uruguay, Portugal, France, Antarctic and Australia have come a rash of reports of so-called unidentified objects. The UFO reports have been the most

> numerous since 1957. Aug, 2: Washington, D.C. "People who thought they were seeing flying saucers last weekend probably were seeing stars," the Air Force announced Monday. It investigated reports of unidentified flying objects over Texas, New Mexico, Oklahoma and Kansas on Saturday and Sunday. Sightings were also reported in Colorado, South Dakota, Nebraska and Wyoming. Aug. 4: Oklahoma City Thousands of persons across the Nation's midlands and Southwest again last night reported seeing mysterious flashes, winking and sparkling phenomena that sped and sometimes zigzagged across the skies. An Air Force weather observer in Oklahoma City has repeatedly seen unusual objects in the skies, and said they are "no mirage". One of the objects "looked like it had a flat top and flat bottom, and it was not a true sphere", the observer said. "There were two rings around it and the rings were part of the main body!"

So the saucer intelligences once again confirmed that I was their representative, and in communication with them.

Next, on August 6, 1965, I wrote George Clark, CIA (plus my other contacts, scientists, government agencies, etc.) as follows:

> Now, for your amusement, and because you've been so good to listen to me for so long, I will let you in on something. I am calling fleets of UFO's here, to Philadelphia, from everywhere. Trouble is I do not know what they can do to prove to these people here that I'm for real. But I will think of something. I believe they are here already, because I sent for them this afternoon. With all that power, whatever kind it is, that they have - and it seems to be miraculous, judging from what they've accomplished this past year - they should do something startling. Am trying to convey the idea to them of coming right down over the city and hovering. But they give me the idea back that we might have some kind of rays like

they have, or whatever it is they have, and hurt them or something, so that they are reticent to do this. So I am trying to tell them we haven't any such thing, and that it's safe for them to appear.

The confirming answer from the UFO's came on Jan. 12, 1966.

Front page newspaper write-ups follow:

UFO SIGHTED AT WANAQUE

(New Jersey ...not far from Philadelphia, where I lived).

FLYING SAUCER CASTS SPOTLIGHT ON RAMAPO AREA by Cecilia King, (Newark, New Jersey Evening News Correspondent):

An unidentified flying object - "very white, very bright and much bigger than a star" hovered silently over this astounded Ramapo countryside for hours last night. Hundreds of eye-witnesses in a 20-mile periphery testified to seeing a flying saucer, first in Oakland, later of the Wanaque Reservoir where it lingered longest, then above Lakeland Regional High School, and finally over the Houdaile sandpit in Haskell. From there it appeared to move southeast towards Pines Lake in Wayne and suddenly disappear.

"The phenomena was terribly strange" Mayor Harry Wolfe said, having been alerted by local police that a UFO was circling over Raymond Dam at the Wanaque head works. Wolfe drove there to see for himself. With him were Councilmen Arthur Barton and Warren Hagstrom, and the mayor's 14-year-old son, Billy. Billy spotted the unidentified object at once. Flying low it glided "oddly" he said. "But it didn't flicker. It was just a continuous light that changed from white to red to green and back to white."

The older observers estimated "the oval" was between two and nine feet in diameter. First word of the terrestrial visitor reached the New Jersey police station in Pompton Lakes at 6:30 P.M. After some 30 telephone calls from excited residents and motorists, the radio monitor contacted Wanaque Patrolman Joseph Cisco.

People in Oakland, Ringwood, Paterson, Totawa, Wayne and Butler claim there's a flying saucer over the Wanaque, he was informed. Cisco radioed reservoir Patrolman George Dykman, and even as Dykman was receiving the message two excited teenagers came running. "Look, look," they pointed excitedly. Dykman gaped along with Michael Sloat, 16, and Peter Melegrae, 15, and a few seconds later they were joined by Civil Defense Director Bentley Spencer and CD member Richard Vrooman. "What the heck is it?" exclaimed Dykman. "Never saw anything like it in my life." Spencer proceeded to the top of 1,300 foot long Raymond Dam with reservoir employee Fred Steines. From that vantage point he reported later that he saw "a bolt of light shoot down, as if attracted to the water." He said it looked "like a beam emitted from a porthole".

In the meantime Reservoir Police Lt. George Destito stood guard at the Wanaque entrance gates turning away swarms of pedestrians and scores of cars converging to the scene from north and south in Ringwood Avenue. The "saucer" hovered for more than two hours over the Raymond Dam area before soaring out of sight. It reappeared over Lakeland Regional High School in the Midvale section of the borough. A crowd of photographers and reporters were on the spot, but before any pictures could be taken the mystery object vanished. The reportedly "last good view" was reported in Highland Avenue, Haskell, where volunteer firemen were burning Christmas trees in the Houdaille sand pit.

Police headquarters continued receiving telephone calls, however, all in the same vein of petrified wonder:

"I saw something weird - what is it?"

Another report by Jack Mahon, Journal-American Staff Writer, New York:

What Did They See Hovering Over Jersey? What was the strange flying object that hovered over the Wanaque Reservoir in Northern New Jersey all through the night, baffling police and terrorizing thousands of residents in neighboring townships? The UFO - which is all anyone could call it - was still unidentified today. The police of Wanaque, Wyckoff, Pompton Lakes, Riverdale, Ringwood and Paterson all witnessed the strange bright light, which resembled a disc, as it dipped and rose over the 15-mile-long reservoir from 7:30 p.m. yesterday until early this morning. They didn't know what to call it. Officials at Steward Air Force Base, Newburg, New York, and McGuire Air Base, Wrightstown, New Jersey, said they'd heard of the UFO - but acted as if they wished they hadn't. Both bases clamped a tight lid of silence on the subject and denied they had sent planes to investigate the phenomena.

Patrolman George Dykman, of the Wanaque Reservoir police, first spotted the weird disc about 200 yards from the police station.

"It was very bright," Patrolman Dykman said, "about two feet in diameter and, as it dipped over the dam, a round light about nine feet in diameter was reflected in the water."

Patrolman Charles Theodora said the disc disappeared at 8:30 p.m., but returned about 2:20 a.m. It was motionless for about an hour, then moved back and forth several times.

"It raced about six miles up and down the dam at supersonic speed," said the officer. "At one point it flashed a ray of light on the ice. Patrolman Capana and I drove up to investigate. We found a hole in the ice about 40 to 50 feet in diameter - there is no explaining it. The rest of the dam is covered solid."

Jack Burchill, an aerospace student at N.Y. Institute of Technology, Westbury, Long Island, and Richard Scott Paterson, a student at Stevens Institute of Technology, Hoboken, gave this analysis:

"It doesn't twinkle, so it is not a star. It's too bright to be a planet or celestial body. It gives off its own light. It can't be a helicopter, for it is soundless and appears to move at better than 1000 miles per hour."

Wanaque Mayor Harry T. Wolfe, Civil Defense Director Bentley Spencer, and Howard Ball, suburban editor of the Paterson Evening News, also spotted the UFO. Mr. Ball said:

"I was driving up a hill. I thought it was the planet Venus. Then it looked like an airplane - but it was too low. I don't know what it is - or was."

Neither does anyone else.

So, the SI's did exactly as I had asked them to do on August 6... they came down and hovered for hours, instead of half an hour, to prove they were real. But they came down at Wanaque, New Jersey (not far from Philadelphia) evidently because they did not trust the Philadelphia area. Also, they demonstrated the very ray I had talked about in my August 6 letter to George Clark.

Once again, the SI's had made an appearance directly in answer to my request, to prove their connection with me, and our ability to communicate with each other.

CHAPTER THREE
THE MICHIGAN MONSTER

Now the action began to get faster, and "furiouser".

Here is a copy of the letter I sent to the Editor of the Philadelphia Daily News on August 18, 1965.

> Dear Sir:
>
> In your story, "Blonde Gets Black Eye as 'Thing' Attacks Car", in your 8/17/65 paper, the mother of the girl who was attacked - and they were both in the car during the attack by the seven-foot, 400 lb. "monster" - has the name of Rose Owens. The girl who was attacked, then was named Owens before her marriage.
>
> A strange coincidence.
>
> The Wednesday previously I appeared on the Jack McKinney Show, Station WCAU, here in Philadelphia, and Mr. McKinney was kind enough to read a three-page letter, or message, given to me by the UFO intelligences to pass on to the American people. So what? What is the coincidence? My name is Ted Owens!

Now, for the reader's benefit, I must explain here that the SI's try to tell humans things by making certain actions occur. For instance, one SI craft led a string of police cars not long ago for a long distance (they were following it, and it was making sure that the police cars kept up with it by stopping and waiting for them once in a while). The SI craft led them to Freedom, Pa. Here the SI's were trying to tell the humans, in their own way, that they, and only they, could lead the United States to freedom - freedom from war, from killing, from hate, from drought, etc.

Then the "Michigan Monster" appeared, just days after Jack McKinnery read the SI message over the radio, and attacked a girl whose maiden name was Owens. The incident was sure to get into the papers where I would see it, and I would know the SI's acknowledged gratefully their message getting to the American people over the radio. Sixteen different people had seen the monster, but it didn't really hurt a single person. Therefore the SI's were trying to show by act that they had no harmful intent towards humans. Perhaps you would be interested in the clipping story which appeared in the newspapers.

> BLONDE GETS BLACK EYE AS "THING" ATTACKS CAR
>
> Monroe, Michigan, UPI.
>
> What weighs more than 400 pounds, smells moldy, growls like a mad dog, and dislikes automobiles?
>
> Answer - the Monroe County Monster. That was the latest on the "thing" that has been sighted here and there in Monroe County during the past two months by at least 16 persons, including Christine Van Acker, a 17-year-old blonde.
>
> Miss Van Acker, who goes to a beautician school here, has a black eye she said was inflicted by the monster Friday night.
>
> State police were checking her story and patrolling the area at night northeast of the southern Michigan city. Miss Van Acker gave this story of the encounter :
>
> "I was driving mother, Mrs. Rose Owens, home. Suddenly there was this bump and a hairy arm grabbed me by the

hair. It wasn't human or anything. I tried to go faster but the car stalled."

The girl fainted. Mrs. Owens, who jumped out of the car and ran for help, described the ordeal like this.

"The first I knew there was this bang and an arm came through the window. Christine yelled, 'Mommy, help me! Oh my God, help!' I told her to get the car going... but it stalled. The monster had his paw entwined in her hair and kept banging her head on the side of the car"

(Note: Still it didn't hurt her... this was to make a big new story that would help me in Philadelphia - Owens),

"and I decided the best thing to do was go for help. When I got back with other people, Christine was semi-conscious, and the monster was gone."

The monster was at least seven feet tall, weighed about 400 pounds, and it had a long reach.

It was all covered with black, bristly hair, and towards the end of the hair it was silver. You couldn't see its face, there was so much hair. And it growled. It had a real growl, and definitely was not a bear. Christine said she was sure it was not a bear because bears have fur and this thing had prickly hair like thorns. She also said she was sure it was not a prankster "because nobody human would do anything like that!"

The monster sightings have occurred in Frenchtown and Ashe townships within the last 60 days. One man reported the monster climbed onto his car, and thumped on the roof and fenders before disappearing into the woods. A woman reported she saw the monster and it smelled moldy.

Ted Owens

CHAPTER FOUR
THE GREAT BLACKOUT

Now comes on of the most terrifying predictions I have made. And you, the reader, were in on this one. On October 26, 1965, the SI's got through to me, in their own way (I was at home with my shoes off, relaxing), and they insisted I get dressed, go downtown to Western Union, and send George Clark, of the CIA, the following telegram:

> MR. GEORGE CLARK
> CENTRAL INTELLIGENCE AGENCY
> WASHINGTON 25, D.C.
>
> A RARE WARNING:SI'S IN FURY. SEE COPY LETTER NASA BEFORE GEMINII SIX SHOT. KEEP IN MIND VANISHING AGENA ROCKET. UNLESS U.S. GOVT. COMPLIES WITH SI WISHES, THEY WILL UNLEASH TERRIBLE U.S. CATASTROPHE WITHIN TEN DAYS. DON'T KNOW WHAT THEY HAVE IN MIND. BUT LET THE GOVT. BE WARNED.
>
> P.K. Man (Owens)

What followed, on November 10, 1965...about ten days later?

Let's look at the news headlines for the answer!

> POWER BLACKOUT PARALYZES 7 STATES
>
> (Phila. Inquirer, 11/10/65)...
>
> The effects of the blackout were monumental. New York, the greatest communication center in the world, could not

communicate for hours except by telephone. The presses of all New York morning newspapers were halted. Planes circling New York's two airports were unable to get down and planes on the ground were unable to take off. Radio and radar communications, apparently were blacked out... In many areas of the city the flow of water was suddenly stopped because of the failure of electrically operated pumps...

26 MILLION PLUNGED INTO DARKNESS AS POWER FAILURE AFFECTS SEVEN STATES

(Phila. Inquirer, 11/10/65).

A massive electric power failure plunged New York City, Boston and vast areas of the Northeast back into the days of candlelight on Tuesday, choking traffic and disrupting communications. The blackout, which extended into parts of Canada, was estimated to have hit cities, towns and countryside in which at least 26 million people live.

It was by far the worst blackout that the Nation has ever suffered.

The power blackout over a huge area of the U.S. and Canada was the major story in newspapers around the world.

...the cause of the blackout remained a dark mystery. Several State and Federal agencies, the FBI and Federal Agencies, the Federal Power Commission included, sought the reason for the paralyzing electrical failure.

Experts Ponder ... What Caused It? Could It Recur? Wash. 11/10 UPI:

Docile electricity turned into an uncontrolled monster that defied all man-made barriers.

(Note: You can "see" the SI's "talking" through this article - Owens)

> and crackled through the northeastern United States, knocking out powerhouses and creating a world of darkness for 30 million Americans. The questions Wednesday: How was it unchained? ...Residents of an 80,000 square mile area experienced the extraordinary night without electricity...

And the following article also "talked" the SI message to the American people beautifully!

> BLACKOUT LEAVES PUSH-BUTTON MAN HELPLESS
>
> by Saul Pett
> N.Y. AP
>
> Thirty million people in eight highly developed American States are thrown into black confusion in the year 1965 when men orbit the earth and their spacecraft explore the moon. Rarely has modern man appeared so vulnerable. The thing they told us couldn't happen, happened Tuesday night and all the giants of automation and all the electronic brains of the computers were helpless to stop the power failure that spread through the Northeast. In great and small ways men were stopped, imprisoned, slowed, confused, frightened, exhausted, and defeated by machines that failed.

(Note: rather, by the SI's - Owens)

> ...In hundreds of great and tiny ways, modern pushbutton man had a big hole in his complacency.

And finally, an excellent editorial in the Philadelphia Inquirer that spelled out the message from the SI's that, if they so wished, the entire U.S. would lie helpless before their powers, at any given moment:

> MASSIVE FAILURE

> It was not only the power that failed Tuesday night. It was merely 30 million people who were plunged suddenly into darkness. It was more than just the great metropolises and the smaller cities and towns that lay helpless and paralyzed when the electricity stopped. This worst power failure in history was of far broader scope than one frightful night in one section of the country. A larger failure lies hidden somewhere in the planning - or in the execution of plans - that supposedly had provided foolproof protection to prevent precisely the kind of power blackout that happened. Until the "impossible" happened at approximately 5:30 P.M. Tuesday, it had been generally believed by electrical experts that the wholesale linkage of power lines, tying millions of people in hundreds of communities into a single network, assured that no community in the system would ever be totally without power for long - even, some authorities said, if there were a nuclear attack. Then came the moment of truth - when the lights went out, the elevators stalled, the railroad and subway trains halted, incoming planes were stranded over darkened airports and near one-sixth of the population of the country, including its largest city, found themselves in all kinds of strange and horrifying circumstances.
>
> Never before, anywhere, have so many persons discovered so swiftly how dependent they are upon electrical power in its enormous variety of manifestations. The entire Nation has a stake in the investigation of how it happened.

(Note: the entire Nation has a stake in the outcome - of the SI's trying, so far in vain, to approach the U.S. Government - Owens.)

Not only had I sent the telegram, warning of this huge event, but on October 26, 1965, just about a week before the blackout, I obtained a signed confirmation of a prediction I typed out on that day for Jim Mancini, at Murray-Jason, Inc., in Philadelphia, Pa., as follows:

Oct. 26, 1965

I predict today there will be a major disaster connected with the U.S. and/or Govt. within 10 days. This could be a major weather or natural catastrophe or military (service) catastrophe. It will be terrible.

Ted Owens
Witnessed: (Signed)
Jim Mancini
Murray-Jason, Inc.
1033 S. 53rd St.
Phila., Pa.

I knew that the SI's were going to hit the country with some major catastrophe, and within days, but did not know what form it would take. So, I covered this major catastrophe thoroughly in advance, before the SI's followed up with their usual action, once again pointing up my ability to receive communication from them.

Ted Owens

CHAPTER FIVE
MORE CONFIRMATION

You can see the pattern by now:

SI's communicate with me; I communicate with scientists, U.S. Govt., etc., and the SI action follows - ingenious plan on the part of the SI's to prove their reality; their connection with me, their human agent; and our ability to communicate with each other.

My next proof along this line (I was, meanwhile, doing many other things, which will be covered in a later book) came in a letter I wrote to scientist Roland Swank (plus my other contacts) on Oct. 15, 1966 :

> Dear Roland:
>
> I have just decided to conduct a beauty of an experiment. I am going to ask the SI's to appear publicly by Halloween.

(Note: this gave me 2 weeks - Owens).

As soon as I had written the letters and sent them off, I contacted the SI's (am going to show you how later) and asked them to appear publicly somewhere around Philadelphia before or on Halloween, and get it written up in the newspapers, preferably on the front pages. I also asked them to appear over a crowded football stadium, where they could be seen by thousands (Note: It turned out they did not choose to do it that way - Owens).

Two weeks went by, and nothing appeared in the papers. The day of Halloween, I scanned the papers, watched TV, and listened to the radio. Nothing. I was deeply disappointed, because this would be the first time they had let me down with confirming proof. The next day, however, while walking downtown in Philadelphia, I passed a newsstand and just happened to glance at a stack of papers. There on the front page of the Courier-Post of Camden, New Jersey (just across the river from Philadelphia) was the following clipping:

> UFO REPORTED BY SIX AREA RESIDENTS
>
> Along with the normal number of Halloween hobgoblins, witches and devils on the ground last night, there may have been something eerie going on in the sky. The Courier-Post received a number of calls about a "long, cigar-shaped object" moving across the sky toward Philadelphia between 6 and 8 p.m. Mrs. Marion Rheine of 25 Beaver Avenue, Barrington, said, "It looked like a blimp. It was cigar-shaped, and a blue light was coming from it. It was going toward Philadelphia, and it was going pretty fast, like it was shot."
>
> Thomas Jones of 312 Lafayette Drive, Mount Ephraim, also described it as a cigar-shaped object heading toward Philadelphia

(Note: where I live, and send out signals to the SI's - Owens.)

> "It had a yellowish-bluish glow and moved faster than any plane," he said, "It made no noise."
>
> Bob Sibley, 35 Remington Avenue, Mount Ephraim, gave the same description but added a red light.
>
> Norman Scott, 149 Linden Avenue, Woodlynne, confirmed the description and said the long tube was making sharp turns in a northwesterly direction toward Philadelphia.
>
> A caller who wished to remain anonymous said the object was "pole-shaped with points on each end, and making no sound". One final anonymous caller cried: "I saw one! I know something's gonna happen! We're all gonna die!"

Therefore the SI's did not let me down. They did exactly as I requested of them, appearing on Halloween, and then in such a fashion that it would be reported on the front page of the Camden paper (Note: Not a word appeared in the Philadelphia papers, to show the control of somebody who must be interested in keeping this from the public - Owens).

I jumped a bit with my dates, but no matter. Another confirmation the SI's went to a great bit of trouble to give me, to convince humans that I was their representative, came in a letter I wrote to Roland Swank on August 13, 1966. I made some predictions in the letter, then stated:

> Furthermore, they (the SI's) will sign their signature to this, by making another startling public appearance, as they did recently at Erie. This appearance, made some time during the above-mentioned period of time, will confirm again that they are indeed bringing all this about, and that I am their representative.

On August 19, six days later, the following article appeared in the newspapers:

> HUNDREDS SCARED BY BRIGHT METEOR
>
> Pittsburg, Pa., Aug. 19, UP:
>
> A meteor so bright that it cast shadows flashed through the sky over western Pennsylvania and Ohio early on Friday, frightened hundreds of persons. Spokesmen at the Allegheny Observatory and the Buhl Planetarium in Pittsburgh said the meteor was of a brightness measured at minus-six magnitude, "the brightest possible". "It lit up the area like a flashbulb" the spokesman said.
>
> Pittsburg police reported receiving more than 250 telephone calls within 20 minutes of the meteor's passing.

The SI's, therefore, gave me their signal of confirmation in this instance.

Ted Owens

CHAPTER SIX
A SAUCER NAMED "FLOYD"

And now, dear reader, you will be utterly astonished at the following action. And you will have to pay close attention.

On June 1, 1966, I sent this letter to George Clark, of the CIA:

> Dear George:
>
> The SI's today gave me some interesting information to pass on. Seems that when they flew near some police cars, in a recent sighting, the stupid policemen actually fired guns at their craft (This was not made public, and may even be kept a secret by the officers who committed this colossal blunder). However, the SI's warn that if they approach in friendly fashion in the future, and are fired upon or attacked in an unfriendly manner, the police will be minus one police car and officers. The SI's will eliminate it, as a lesson to humans.

Remember that letter, readers, it is important.

Oct. 1, 1966, several months later, the following newspaper article appeared, and the police officers involved in the encounter with the SI's did in fact disappear from the police force! This after my letter predicting it!

> Flying Saucer Named Floyd Is Man's Eternal Tormentor
>
> by John De Groot, Akron Beacon Journal

Staff Writer, Akron Ohio

In his ruined world of loneliness and twisted nightmares, Dale Spur wonders if the chase will ever end. It began six months ago, with seven steps to hell and a flying saucer named Floyd. In the predawn hours of the gentle April morning, Spaur, a Portage County sheriff's deputy, chased a flying saucer 86 miles. Now the strange craft is chasing him. And he is hiding from it, a bearded stranger peering past the limp curtains of a tiny motel room in Solon, Ohio.

He is no longer a deputy sheriff. His marriage is shattered. He has lost 40 pounds. He lives on one bowl of cereal and a sandwich each day. He walks three miles to an $80 a week painter's job. His motel room costs $60 a week. The court has ordered him to pay his wife $20 a week for the support of his two children. That leaves Dale Spaur exactly nothing. The flying saucer did it.

"If I could change all that I have done in my life," he said, "I would change just one thing. And that would be the night I chased that damn thing. That saucer."

He spit the word out. Saucer. An obscenity. Others might understand. Four other officers took part in the April drama.

(Note: Which, I wonder, shot at the saucer? - Owens)

Police Chief Gerald Buchert of Mantua saw the craft and photographed it The pictures turned out badly, an odd fuzzy white thing suspended in blackness. Today, Chief Buchert laughs nervously when he speaks of that night.

"I'd rather not talk about it," he says. "It's something that should be forgotten and left along. I saw something, but I don't know what it was."

Special Deputy W.L Neff rode with Spaur during the chase. He won't talk about it. His wife, Jackelyne, explains

"I hope I never see him like he was after the chase. He was real white, almost in a state of shock. It was awful. And people made fun of him afterwards. He never talks about it anymore. Once he told me

'If that thing landed in my backyard, I wouldn't tell a soul.'

He's been through a wringer."

Patrolman Frank Panzanella saw the chase end in Conway, Pa., where he works. He saw the craft. Now he is silent. Friends say he had his telephone removed.

He tells you:

"Sure I quit because of that thing. People laughed at me. And there was pressure. You couldn't put your finger on it, but the pressure was there. The city officials didn't like police officers chasing flying saucers."

As to the other officers, three still wear badges, but do not speak of what they saw. Spaur and Huston have turned in their badges.

(Note: thus two were eliminated, as per my earlier prediction - Owens).

Now Spaur hides in Solon, a fugitive from a flying saucer named Floyd. He cannot escape the strange craft. It remains with him, locked in his mind, reappearing in nightly sweating dreams that are a bizarre mixture of reality and fantasy.

Of that night: He is driving car 13. Barney Neff is beside him. They are heading east along U.S. 224 between Randolf and Atwater when they spot a red and white 1959 Ford alongside the road. Barney and Dale stop to check it out. The car is filled with walkie-talkies and other radios. A strange emblem is painted on the side. A triangle with a bolt of lightning inside it. Above the emblem is written "Seven Steps to Hell".

(Note: This is tremendously important, although it meant nothing to the authorities. For several years my own emblem I have used to sign my letters to scientists and government agencies, has been a large "O" with a line through the center, and a lightning bolt underneath the "O". As I interpret this message from the SI's, a "step" is a time interval and after seven of these time intervals, or "steps", the U.S. will be destroyed. They, the SI's, are trying to stop our being destroyed. - Owens.)

Suddenly Spaur hears a humming sound behind him. He turns and sees a huge, saucer-shaped craft rising out of a woods. The entire underside of the craft gleams with an intense, purplish-white light. Spaur calls to Barney, who turns, sees the craft, then stands paralyzed.

Neither moves. Spaur is sure he can't move. That his limbs do not work. He does not know why he is sure of this. He just believes it. The ship rises to about 150 feet and moves directly over the patrol car. Both men feel warm, pleasing heat from the bottom of the craft, but the light is so intense that tears stream from their eyes. Spaur thinks about moving back to the car. Yet he does not. Some trace of a thought which seems to tell him that if he touches the car it will disappear.

(Note: see my letter written before this article appeared: "Will be minus one police car." - Owens)

Then the saucer moves away from the car and stops. As though on command, both men race to the cruiser. Later, Spaur thinks that is strange, that both would move at exactly the same instant. Spaur radios in, telling the deskman what he has seen. Other reports have already flared over the radio. "Shoot it" the radio man tells Spaur.

(Note: Remember now, my letter warning about this was written well before this article appeared! - Owens)

Again, some strange feeling tells Spaur not to get out of the cruiser and shoot at the craft. It is about 50 feet across and maybe 15 to 20 feet high. On top of it is a large dome. An antenna juts out from the rear part of the dome. The night sergeant comes on the radio and tells Spaur to chase it. The craft moves away and Spaur follows. Slowly at first. Later, he hits speeds of more than 100 miles and hour racing eastward through Ohio and Pennsylvania. The craft seems to be letting Spaur follow it. It waits for him at intersections. Once, it seems to double back when he is forced to turn away from its eastward path. Finally, after the sun has risen, the chase ends near Pittsburgh, when Spaur runs out of gas. That is what happened, according to Spaur and Neff.

Now Spaur relives the chase each night in a twisting nightmare. But in his dream, car 13 vanishes. Disappears when he touches it. And then Spaur stands alone beneath the huge ship. At this moment he awakens shivering and wet. Alone in his motel room. As he speaks of the six months since he saw the flying saucer named Floyd, it is difficult to tell when the nightmare stops and reality begins. Spaur does not know what happened to the sedan with "Seven Steps to Hell" written on its sides. After the chase, his daily routine was washed away in a sea of reporters, television cameramen, Air Force investigators, government officials, strange letters from places like Little Rock, Ark., and Australia that told him what to do if the "little green men" tried to contact him.

"My entire life came crashing down around my shoulders" he said. "Everything changed. I still don't really know what happened. But suddenly it was as though everybody owned me and I no longer had anything for myself. My wife, my home, my children. They all seemed to fade away."

Spaur's wife Daneise now is alone with their two children. She has filed for divorce and is working as a waitress in a bar at Ravenna.

"Something happened to Dale, but I don't know what it was" she says. "He came home that day and I never saw him more frightened before. He acted strange, listless. He just sat around. He was very pale. Then later, he got real nervous. And he started to run away. He's just disappear for days and days. I wouldn't see him. Our marriage fell apart. All sorts of people came to the house. Investigators, reporters. They kept him up all night. They kept after him, hounding him. They hounded him right into the ground. And he changed."

Then one night, Dale came home very late. He isn't sure what happened. He walked into the living room. There were some other people there. Things were very tense. Very confused. He grabbed his wife and shook her. Hard. He kept shaking her. It left big ugly bruises on her arms. He doesn't know how or why. That was the end of July. Daneise filed assault and battery charges. Dale was jailed, and turned in his badge. A newspaper printed a story about the deputy who chased the flying saucer being jailed for beating his wife. When he got out of jail, Dale left town, turned his back on everything. But the saucer followed him, locked in his dreams. In Ravenna, Daneise can only say

"Dale is a lost soul. And everything is finished for us."

In Solon, Dale said, "I have become a freak. I'm so damn lonely. Look at me, 34 years old and what do I have?

Nothing. Who knows me? To everyone I am Dale Spaur, the nut who chased a flying saucer. My father called me several weeks ago. A long time ago we had a fight. I hadn't heard from him for years. Then he calls me. Do you think he called to ask how I was, to say I love you, son, to see if I wanted to go fishing or something? Hell no. He wanted to know if I'd seen any more flying saucers. I tried to go to church for help. I went to church and the minister introduced me to the congregation. 'We have the man who chased a flying saucer with us today,' he said."

Dale Spaur wept s he told what the flying saucer named Floyd had done to him. He calls it Floyd because he saw it once more while he was still working for the sheriff's department.

The radio operators knew civilians were monitoring their broadcasts so they agreed to use a code name if the flying saucer was seen again. They called it Floyd, Dale Spaur's middle name.

Dale was driving east on Interstate 80-S one night in June. He looked up. There it was.

"Floyd's here with me" he whispered into the radio. Then he parked the car, and sat there, alone. This time Barney Neff was not with him. Dale did not look out the window. He lit a cigarette and stared at the floor of the cruiser. He sat there for nearly 15 minutes not looking outside, not wanting to see Floyd.

When he looked up, Floyd had disappeared. Yet it still follows him. And it has ruined his life. This he believes.

Well, reader, I wonder which one shot at the saucer? That was a mistake. There is now way, no human way, that we can injure or destroy the saucers. But the SI's have let me know that they fear our attacks, our attempts to snare their craft, by any means. Not because we might do so - we cannot - but because there is some law of their own, something about them, that reflects our "get them, destroy them" thought back onto us, destroying us... perhaps not physically, but in other, worse ways.

Such as Dale Spaur.

CHAPTER SEVEN
SAUCERS OVER PHILADELPHIA

Now we come to one of my hottest, best predictions of when and where a UFO would appear, as told me by the SI's themselves. And if you live on the East Coast, you know all about its appearance. It was reported in big national magazines and on the front pages of newspapers after it appeared.

On April 19, 1966, I wrote George Clark, CIA, and all my contacts, as follows:

> Dear George:
>
> Something momentous is in the wind with the SI's. So big, that they are actually going to attempt to bring one of their craft down into Philadelphia to contact me! One of the big ones, that is.
>
> For some time I have been trying to get them to do just that, but not until today did they signal that they were going to come into Philadelphia - into Center City - to try a contact with me.
>
> That is how important it is to them to make a contact physically with their human contact. I understand from "thinking with them" that ordinarily they hate to go into a city, down around buildings, etc. But, frustrated over the U.S. Government's refusal to help me meet them in the Michigan woods, or in an isolated European castle, - they will make an effort to find me, here.

> They know where I am at all times, but reaching me with one of their large craft, that's something else. So, when you read about the UFO seen in Philadelphia, in the days or weeks ahead, you will know who it is linking up with.

In the days that followed, the feeling that the SI's were drawing closer pressed in on me, so on Saturday afternoon, late, I actually dashed down to South Street in Philadelphia, to the pawn shops, to buy a camera to take a picture of the UFO when it came. But due to the late hour I had to buy one at Peerless Camera, in Center City. Sunday, nothing happened, but I kept the camera handy. Monday nothing happened, but I took the camera to work, just in case. Monday evening we were eating supper when the news hit TV and radio. The UFO had appeared! While I was indoors, dammit! Here is the fascinating account:

> FLAMING METEOR SEEN OVER PHILADELPHIA
>
> April 26, 1966 (by David M. Cleary, of the Bulletin Staff):
>
> A flaming object, apparently a meteor of unusually large size, streaked through the skies over Philadelphia just after 6 p.m. last night. Seen by thousands of people, it was blue-green in color, with a fiery red-orange tail, and was visible for about 15 seconds. It was seen in a trajectory that began in eastern North Carolina, as it apparently came in from over the Atlantic Ocean, to Ottawa, Canada, where pilots about to land described it "going in a northwest by north direction, and probably landed just north of here". But the sightings were also reported over a wide east-west band, as far east as Boston and as far west as eastern Ohio, indicating that the meteor was much higher than it appeared to be from any one observation point and therefore much larger.
>
> Dr. Thomas D. Nicholson, of the Hayden Planetarium in New York, said, "It was at least 100 times brighter than Venus when that planet is at its greatest brilliance, and

about 10,000 times brighter than Sirius (the Dog Star) which is the brightest star we see at night."

Some astronomers said, shortly after the meteor passed, that it was probably a tiny meteorite, perhaps no larger than a football, that was burning itself out as it plunged through the atmosphere toward earth. But that opinion weakened as reports of the meteor were made from so many points to the east and west of its path. Since it was visible from points 300 miles or so to each side of its path, it must have been at least 50 miles high, and perhaps as far as 100 miles.

I saw it as I was walking north on 36th Street approaching Walnut, having just left the Wistar Institute at 36th and Spruce Sts. after a ten-hour session devoted to mathematical challenges of Darwin's 1859 theory of evolution. I was walking with William Bossert, PhD., a mathematician, with the computation laboratories at Harvard University, who had been a speaker during the evolution symposium. We both saw the meteor very clearly and for a period of about 15 seconds.

My watch gave the time as 8:06 p.m. "The strange thing about the meteor, said Dr. Bossert, was the brilliance of its light was constant during the time we observed it. That could only mean that it was traveling at approximately the orbital velocity of five miles a second and was moving parallel to the spherical surface of the earth, rather than falling toward the earth. Had it been moving toward the earth," Dr. Bossert pointed out, "it would have increased in brilliance as it encountered increasing density of atmosphere, then faded as it burned itself out."

Hold on, now, readers, and follow this particular case through, because you are going to be in for a real surprise when you discover that the SI's really kept their promise. Another article re the "Fireball" was written by Robert J. Hayes, of the Philadelphia Inquirer Staff, and dated April 26, 1966.

> THOUSANDS SIGHT "FIREBALL"
>
> A bright ball of fire trailing a long fiery tail startled thousands in the Delaware Valley and most of the Mid-Atlantic Coast as it shot across the sky near sundown Monday. The object, reported seen in Rochester, N.Y., Boston, in areas of Ohio and the Carolinas, was described soon after it was sighted by astronomers and Federal Aviation Agency authorities as the meteor. Dr. I.M. Levitt, director of the Franklin Institute's Fels Planetarium, said the fireball was seen by a member of his staff, Edward Bailey, of Bala Cynwyd.
>
> "From his description", Dr. Levitt said, "it was most likely a meteor, but there are too many unknowns". The object, he said, was "very unusual, for two reasons. For one, it was as bright as a full moon. It was also very slow. You can usually count on seeing meteors only for about 15 seconds."
>
> The object, seen about 8:10 p.m., caused a general swamping of area police switchboards. Philadelphia police headquarters alone reported more than 500 calls, many from policemen. Municipal telephones buzzed to the tune of about 1000 calls. Phone calls swamped police boards in Delaware, Montgomery, Chester and Bucks counties and in the North and South New Jersey.
>
> A private pilot landed at the Bridgeport, N.J. airport and reported seeing "a large, brilliantly green spherical object" about 5000 feet in the air going at about 600 miles an hour. "It was headed due west, and extinguished itself in the vicinity of the General Electric plant in Chester."

(Note: My scientist friend, Roland Swank, who received a copy of the prediction six days before this event, works for General Electric - Owens)

Another article stated that

> Flying saucer fears also were rampant, especially, in all probability, since the recent mysterious UFO sightings in Michigan and elsewhere.

A 14-year old boy, Dana DeGeorge, took a fine picture of it from his back yard, in Utica, New York. I looked at the photo he got, and quickly went to Life magazine, which had done a story on UFOs; and sure enough, this boy's picture that he had taken of the "Fireball" was absolutely identical to the photo of a UFO in Life taken by L. Benedek, at Perth, Australia.

And Benedek's description fitted the fireball, too. He says

> I noticed a bright light descending from a great height. It was radiating a light greenish glow and had an exhaust trail of the same color. Its shape, as well as I could judge it, was slightly oval.

All right. So much for that. I knew that the SI's had come over Philadelphia. But they had stated that they would come down in Philadelphia. This puzzled me. Then in August, 1966, Fate Magazine, I got my answer. There was an article that read as follows:

> I never quite believed the stories about UFO's but I believe them now. On April 26, 1966, a balmy evening, three of my neighbors and I sat on the steps talking when suddenly one of the women pointed upward and screamed, "Look! Look!". We all looked skyward - to see a green cone-shaped flying object with fire coming from its tail. The object left a path of smoke like a jet trail or skywriting. We watched it until it was out of sight but the trail of smoke remained for quite a long time. One of the women,

> extremely excitable, wailed, "Oh, it's the end of the world!". But we all managed to calm down and someone suggested we call the newspapers. I did - and the switchboard operator asked me if the call was about "something in the sky".
>
> They were swamped with calls.

(Note: There was not one word about this in the Philadelphia newspapers, to show the control someone has over the news in this city - Owens).

> The radio, TV and newspapers called the object a meteor

(Note: This party got their private UFO confused with the Fireball which appeared the same evening - Owens)

> but I doubted this. The next day I called the Fels Planetarium and the man I reached also insisted that it was a meteor. I asked him if a meteor left a trail of smoke and again he answered "No". I asked him if this were the case, how could he say the object was a meteor? He replied, "Lady, we don't know what it was".

So there, you see, reader, not only did the giant UFO swing over Phila. that evening, but a small one appeared down inside the city itself!

And here is a bit of information no one has. Just last week I was being interviewed by Ida Lewis, well known writer for Jeune Afrique, a French magazine, and she saw this article in Fate Magazine. She exclaimed,

"Why, that's it!".

I asked her what she meant.

"That night of April 26," she explained, "a friend of my mother's called and asked for my brother to come over to her house. He went over, and came back, and said that her house had turned green, and everything in it was green - the silver, the tables, the chairs!"

"Evidently," Miss Lewis added, "it was caused by this green UFO that appeared!"

The next case in which I was involved directly with the UFO was as follows:

In a July 13, 1966, letter to George Clark, CIA, and my other contacts, I made some predictions. At the end of the letter I wrote:

"If they (the SI's) appear publicly now - it will mean I am correct."

The very next day in a newspaper report from Omaha, Nebraska, sightings were reported at Burwell, Ord, Norfolk, Omaha and North Loup-Scotia in Nebraska and at Council Bluffs, Iowa.

> A spokesman for Offutt Air Force Base confirmed it has received three such reports and an investigation was being conducted by the Air Force Systems Command at Wright Patterson Air Force Base in Ohio.

The SI's therefore once more confirmed my writing, by their "appearance" signal.

CHAPTER EIGHT
THE PENINSULA MONSTER

At this point I submit the eeriest, weirdest UFO prediction I have made yet (and remember, if the UFOs did not tell me themselves, how else would I know when, or where they would appear, or what they were going to do?).

In a letter to George Clark and contacts, July 11, 1966, I wrote some predictions, then added:

> The SI's are near this area, and are about to make a move that will bring them to public notice again, just in case people are forgetting them. Something startling. They are getting restless because I am not getting anywhere with the U.S. Government.

How right I was (of course I was, the SI's had told me to write that).

Front Page, The Morning News, Erie, Pa., August 1, 1966:

> UFO SIGHTED ON PENINSULA, GIRL DESCRIBES LANDING
>
> An unidentified flying object was sighted on the Peninsula shortly after dusk Sunday night. A Jamestown, N.Y., girl described by Peninsula police as being almost hysterical, near shock, said a craft suddenly appeared in the night sky from the north and landed about 300 yards from the car she was sitting in. She was identified as Betty Jean Klem, 359 Brodhead Ave., Jamestown, N.Y. Peninsula police were taking the statement from her and several friends today.

Miss Klem gave the following account to a Morning News reporter:

"We were sitting in the car waiting for help. Our car was stuck in the sand. We saw a star move. It got brighter. It would move fast, then dim. You could see it come down. It was metallic. Sort of silvery. It landed between two trees. It came straight down. The car vibrated. I know we saw it. We had taken a walk up in that area earlier. There was nothing between those trees then. All of a sudden it was just there. We could see the lights on the back."

(She later described the craft as being mushroom shaped with a narrow base rising up to an oval structure.)

The sixteen year old girl was still shaking as she talked to the newsman and police officers. Her eyes were red from crying. Police described her as a pretty sensible young woman.

Peninsula Police Chief Dan Dasconio said, "I know what people are going to say, but this girl saw something that scared her badly. This is no joke as far as I'm concerned."

The girl said that as she and her boyfriend, Douglas J. Tibbets, eighteen, of Greenhurst, N.Y., watched from the front seat of his car a beam of light came out of the craft and moved along the ground in a straight line.

"It lit up the whole woods along its path. It wasn't like a search light. There was light along the ground, along its whole path."

She said the light did not waver back and forth like a search light, but continued to extend its beam into the woods. Shortly after the light went into the woods, there occurred the most horrible part of her ordeal, according to the girl. She related that a Peninsula police car approached from behind and pulled up near their stuck vehicle. She said as it did so the beam from the UFO light went out. Her boyfriend jumped from the car and told the officers, "There's something weird going on here."

The officer accompanied the youths down the road about 300 yards to a point near where they said the craft had landed. Just as they approached the area the horn sounded in the boy friend's car and they ran back.

The girl said there was a "thing right by the car. I don't know what it was. It was bigger than you," she told the newsman. It was about six feet tall. "You would have had to look up to see it."

In a very brief sketch that the girl drew of the "Thing" it appeared to have the general shape of an upright, large creature, such as a gorilla, although she maintained it was not any kind of animal that she has ever seen before. She described it as a dark, apparently featureless creature, not human, maybe animal, which moved sluggishly back into the bush after she had leaned on the horn after seeing it.

In her interview by the Morning News, she made the following comments: "The ship was big. It came half-way up between these trees." (Officials said the trees are 60 to 70 feet tall).

"When it came down and landed, the car vibrated. We had the car radio on. I think it was WICU Radio. No, it didn't make any interference on the radio."

(Note: The SI's have explained to me that when they come down to examine a car or vehicle, or a town, they throw out a "web" of power which knocks out electricity, car batteries, radios, etc., so that whatever they are examining cannot escape, or radio or signal by mechanical means for help. Evidently in this case they had reason not to project such a power-web. Owens)

> Asked if it made any kind of noise, she said, "It sounded like the noise in a telephone receiver, only louder, of course. Then it stopped. When it landed there were no lights on it. Then some lights came on by the back of it. The oval top. The others asked me if I saw it. We just couldn't believe it was really happening."
>
> At one point during the interview, she suddenly said,
>
> "We heard someone walking on the roof. No, it wasn't stomping. It was more like scratching. We didn't see anything then. We didn't get out of the car. I was a nonbeliever about this space craft business. But I believe now."

Things happen fast readers. August 3, two days later, a farmer took a picture of a UFO at New Castle, Pa., which was believed to be the same one seen at Preseque Isle Peninsula, on Aug. 1, by the girl and her friends. Next day, August 2, after the girl and her friends had their encounter, huge claw-prints were found in the sand of a beach nearby. They "were staggered, as if made by a walking creature". Patrolmen said the imprints were five to six feet apart. Later in the day the same imprints were found leading to the water of the lake. Patrolmen were particularly intrigued by the markings on the imprints which appeared to have been made by claws. They said, "It was as if you were to take four fingers and press hard in the sand". Patrolmen were also amazed by the sharpness of the impressions in the soft sand. Scratches and dents were also found on the car the teenagers had been in.

So again, readers, the SI's had told me correctly.

They were going to do something startling...

and they did!

CHAPTER NINE
ANOTHER GREAT BLACKOUT

Now you are going to be a reading witness to one of the darndest modern-day miracles you could ever imagine!

Here is what happened. I finished this book last Sunday, completely. Now, you have read inside about my telegram of warning to the CIA, and how a few days later, the Great Blackout of New York took place, two hours ago. Very well. The day after I finished this book (last Monday), the Great Daytime Blackout struck Pennsylvania, New Jersey, Maryland and Delaware! Was any of it my doing? I'll say it was - and I'll let you be the judge, as you follow the action:

> June 21, 1966
>
> Mr. Jack McKinney
> Radio Station WCAU
> Philadelphia, Pa.
>
> Dear Jack:
>
> I have been fighting off writing this to you for several weeks, but when the SI's put on the pressure...you write. What they want me to do is to give a practical demonstration at Radio Station WCAU of how 'PK' (SI power) works at Cape Kennedy and other places. This will involve making a 'PK' map, my usual procedure (the SI's use this as a training procedure with me, so that I can understand what they are doing). I will send you a copy, and keep a copy of this map. Then slowly the power will

build up at Radio Station WCAU as the 'PK' grows there. And in the days, weeks, and months ahead, this is what to expect:

High degree of human error.

Electrical disturbances and breakdowns.

Electromagnetic disturbances.

Fires.

Poltergeist phenomena of all kinds.

Lightning hits.

Employees out with the "flu".

Markedly unreasonable human behavior.

Mechanical malfunction.

Weird and unusual accidents of minor nature.

The SI's are keeping in mind that WCAU, and Jack McKinney, are their friends, so don't worry about this being devastating, as their work is at other places. They just want to show WCAU what it is really like to be within range of the SI's for a period of time, with the SI's zeroing in, that is. Let me spell it out: they are punishing the Air Force currently, with blood in their eye. This is not the same. They are giving WCAU a practical demonstration in SI Pk, with friendship in their eye.

Sincerely,

P K Man (Owens)

Now, you will notice the reference to a lightning hit in the letter. Following is a letter I received in response to an inquiry I made:

KYW Radio
1619 Walnut Street
Philadelphia, Pa.

August 23, 1966

Dear Mr. Owens:

Thank you for your letter dated August 17, 1966. Yes, we were hit by lightning about 2:50 A.M. and we were off the air until temporary repairs could be made, returning to the air at 8:06:30 A.M. ..

(Signed)E.J. Commings

Chief Engineer

So the SI's struck a local radio station with lightning not long after I sent them the PK map. Why not WCAU? I don't know.

Of course, when the Great Daytime Blackout struck, it clobbered WCAU Radio and TV.

Next, on Feb. 19, 1967, I wrote Tim Beckley, Editor of Searchlight, 3 Courtland Street, New Brunswick, New Jersey:

Dear Tim:

...You requested I ask the SI's to furnish good weather for your UFO meeting in New York. This I cannot do, for the SI's have the U.S. set up for rain and precipitation, to eliminate the drought, and this we would not want to tamper with. But, this we can do, I will contact the SI's immediately, and ask them to appear strongly in the New York area through the UFO meeting, to draw attention to New York area, and to them. I'll stress as best I can to them that they do something unusually spectacular at the time of the UFO meeting - like another total New York blackout, or something of that scope. I trust this will meet with your group's approval. One important thing, and please let me know. If I bring the above about, which will certainly help your UFO meeting, will you give me a notarized confirmation of it?

(Note: This was done, and I will exhibit it later - Owens)

Meanwhile I wrote another letter to Roland Swank,

Organization of Scientific Research, Box 562, Paoli, Pa.,

Feb. 23, 1967:

Dear Roland:

Just to jog things up a little, am going to contact the SI's and ask them to bring down, all over the U.S., a blanket of electrical interference, to interfere with telephone wires and connections, radios, TV's, etc., on a mass scale which will be quite noticeable, in an unprecedented way, and which should make the newspapers. Electrical interference and havoc now, all over the U.S. Ready?

P K Man (Owens)

Well, it came to pass, culminating in the Great Daytime Blackout of four East Coast States. But let's look at some of the lesser ones.

Feb. 25, 1967 (two days after the above letter was written), a Philadelphia paper:

NINE SIRENS GO BERSERK

Nine air raid sirens, perched atop utility poles in the Tioga-Nicetown section, went berserk Friday night, wailing for 25 minutes... the wailings stirred up neighborhoods and flooded police telephone lines. A woman at the Electrical Bureau, when asked about the cause, replied "We are not permitted to give out any information."

Next,

> GULF COAST HIT BY POWER FAILURE, Beaumont, Tex., May 11 UP:
>
> A power failure knocked out electricity along the upper Texas Gulf Coast on Friday. At least a quarter of a million persons in the oil-rich cities of Beaumont, Port Arthur, Nederland, Orange and Port Neches were affected. Almost all radio and television stations were knocked off the air, and in some cases telephone communications were interrupted.

Check my letter once again, and you will see that this is exactly what I had asked the SI's to bring about.

Then,

> POWER IS RESTORED IN CINCINNATI AFTER CITY'S ALL-NIGHT BLACKOUT, Cincinnati, May 27, N.Y. Times:..
>
> The blackout, which occurred at about 11:45 PM last night, plunged most of Cincinnati and parts of neighboring Kentucky across the river into blackness.. Henry Sandman, Cincinnati Safety Director, said both the city and the power company were investigating the power failure which he termed highly unusual if it were an accident.

(Note: This blackout was laid to a broken cable over a river, but the reader must bear in mind that the SI's will employ endless means to bring about an effect. They are not limited in any way to their ways of attack, even breaking cables - Owens).

Then,

> MISHAP AROUSES CAPITAL SUBURBS, Washington, June 5, UP:

> Hundreds of residents in two suburbs of the Nation's capital awoke early Monday to the wailing of air raid sirens. The sirens began sounding in parts of Alexandria and Arlington, Va., at 4:30 AM... A Civil Defense spokesman said the sirens were accidentally triggered by a "malfunction of telephone equipment!"

(Note: It was later in this same day that the Great Daytime Blackout occurred - Owens)

My next letter to Roland Swank, C.S.C.A.R., as follows, April, 8, 1967:

> Dear Roland:
>
> An idea has come to me. Am asking the SI's to prove their existence further, and their link with me further, by doing the following: To interfere with TV reception on this entire area, Phila. and nearby New Jersey. Am asking them to make it so outstanding that it will be noted and reported to the authorities by many many people, and thus confirm this letter.
>
> This will also prove their control over television principles, thence over human minds.

Well, I had something a bit different in mind with that letter, but evidently the SI's chose an entire blackout, which certainly fulfilled the letter, also, as the other, previous letters were brought to pass.

Meanwhile I had made a PK map of the Philadelphia - New Jersey - New York area, with appropriate symbols on it, and showed it to the SI's. Next on May 9, 1967, I got a card from Jim Moseley, Chairman of the Flying Saucer Convention in New York, and Editor of Saucer News, as follows:

> Dear Mr. Owens:
>
> I have just finished fixing up your ad for our forthcoming Summer issue of Saucer News. We are also including your

letter to the Editor, about possible sensational activity by the space people, just before the Convention.

(Note that "just before" - Owens)

Yes, that would be wonderful. If you can arrange it! Let's see if you can.

Jim Moseley

I immediately answered Jim's letter as follows, on May 10, 1967:

Dear Jim:

Thanks for the card. Am contacting the SI's immediately to do something sensational in their area of activity

(Note: by that I meant was contacting them over and over again, just to make sure - Owens)

to point up the (Flying Saucer) convention and draw interest to it.

(Note: This was brought to pass, because a local TV Station, WKBS, had received copies of these predictions, as had WCAU Radio, and they both asked me to appear after the Daytime Blackout on their shows, at which time I plugged the Convention - Owens)

I will explain to them that this Convention is in their interest, and the people attending it who are sympathetic to them. Am going to ask them to bring about another Great Power Blackout, or something on that scale. And if they will not do that, then to appear in great numbers in and about New York from now until Convention time, as a signal that they are here, are real, and wish the humans in the U.S. to focus their attention on the Convention. Fair enough? My batting average thus far, which Mack McKinney states is "amazing", is 88%. So am not worried the SI's might not respond.

P K Man (Ted Owens)

Jim Moseley answered on May 17, 1967, as follows:

Dear Ted Owens:

Thanks for your letters. It's very interesting how you have apparently made many of your predictions come true. I would be most sincerely impressed if you can, indeed, make something spectacular happen just before the Convention.

(Note: There it is again, "just before the Convention". The SI's struck with their massive blackout just as requested by Jim, just before the Convention - Owens)

Let's not have a power failure in NYC too close to the Convention date, however, as people might get scared or something.

(Note: 17 days before, was just about right, and right to Jim's order - Owens)

(Signed) Jim Moseley

Just to make sure there would be no misunderstanding, I wrote Jim back on May 19, 1967, as follows:

Dear Jim:

Am asking the SI's to deal NY another power blackout, or show their craft there in a striking way, or do something big and mysterious, before June 22, in NY, to help boost interest in the Convention. Am sure you will get powerful results. Something exciting and unusual. Should affect power and electricity, when it happens.

P K Man (Ted Owens)

Two days after this letter, the following appeared in the New York Times:

> ST. ALBANS BLACKED OUT, St. Albans section of Queens was blacked out for nearly an hour and a half last night...

On May 22, 1967, I wrote Jim back, pointed out this small blackout to him, and telling him, "This seems to be a beginning."

He sent me a card back to answer:

> Thanks for the letter.
> I'll look forward to the blackout!
> Jim Moseley.

On June 5th the massive power failure struck! I immediately sent a telegram to Moseley (after the power came back on) as follows:

> You said "I'll look forward to the blackout."
> I gave it to you. May I have confirmation, please?
> Ted Owens

Now, I would like to show you, the reader, some quotes from the newspapers, regarding the massive Blackout.

The Philadelphia Inquirer called it a "mysterious power failure". It said,

> The big question - why did it happen - could not be answered immediately. Pennsylvania - New Jersey - Maryland Interconnection, PJM, is equipped with switches that are supposed to disconnect generators of transmission lines from the system if trouble develops. In this instance, however, the entire system shut down. Three widely separated generating stations stopped functioning.

Roy G. Rinclife, chairman of Philadelphia Electric, said (before the blackout),

> It is highly improbable that a total blackout could strike our service area.

The Editor of the Inquirer said

> When electric power suddenly was shut off in the memorable blackout on Nov. 9 1965, extensive investigations were launched and preventive measures were taken, supposedly, to avert a repetition of a power failure over such a wide area.

Congressman Fred Rooney said

> It is particularly important to undertake a special study because the power failure centered on the Pennsylvania-New Jersey-Maryland Interconnection is regarded as a "model" for electric power nets.

So you see, dear reader, the SI's knocked out what was regarded as the "model", the best of all U.S. power nets!

Next came Jim Moseley's confirmation, bless his heart. I say that because most of my contacts have for years denied me confirmations, because of fear of possible academic reaction, or Government pressure, or social pressure...who knows? But Jim had guts.

> Dear Ted
>
> I am sorry you had to spend money on telegrams, as I would have written you anyhow, commenting on the success of your prediction regarding the Convention. Your letter to Tim Beckley, published in our current Summer issue of Saucer News, reads as follows:
>
> "I will be contacting the Saucer Intelligence immediately, and ask them to appear strongly in the New York area throughout the UFO Convention, to draw attention to New York and to themselves. I'll stress as best I can to them that they should do something unusually spectacular at that

time, like another New York blackout, or something of that scope. I trust that this will meet with your group's approval".

I do not have the exact date of the above letter, but it was written before May 10th, as our issue went to press at that time. The Convention in question is scheduled for June 23-25. The recent four-state blackout, apparently centering on Philadelphia, took place on June 5th, and extended as far north as Jersey City, directly across the Hudson River from New York. Although there is certainly no proof, one way or the other,

(Note: What better proof could there be, than my many letters written just previously, stating I would specifically work to make this happen with SI help? - Owens),

that the blackout was caused by the prediction, our group is nevertheless very impressed with the closeness, in time and location, regarding the outcome of this prediction.

(Signed) Jim Moseley

Just one more point to explain, dear reader. Several days after the blackout the SI's contacted me, and explained why they did not black out New York itself. To do that they would have had to go over New York, and at the time, although they felt it was the right time, they suspected that, because of my copies of letters to Government agencies, the Government might have set a trap over New York. So they did the next best thing and blacked out the entire adjoining four-state area to make their point.

Ted Owens

CHAPTER TEN
HOW YOU CAN CONTACT THE SI'S

Well, dear readers, enough of all this. I hope you are convinced by now that I have, and can, communicate at will with flying saucers. If there are any among you who can predict UFO appearances in a certain area, and it does occur there within a few days, or even a couple of weeks, then I will believe you.

So we will now pass on to the actual means of communication - what you bought the book for - so that pperhaps you, too, can communicate with the SI's. But I have to teach you a certain way. The best way to begin is to tell you how I started.

In water-witching, a forked twig is held in the hands, and experts find water with it. In my rain-making, and causing lighting to strike, a certain technique is used. I extend my fingers at the skies, and visualize in my mind's eye lightning reaching from my fingers up into the sky. On the sky itself I superimpose, in my mind's eye, the words, "Rain, storm, thunder, lightning". I sense that the lightning from my fingers will cause storm conditions, and crystallize them for the finished product. In my mind's eye I see silent, motionless trees being bent almost double by powerful wind, and I again see, superimposed over the sunny landscape, black sheets of rain beating down.

After doing this for 10 to 20 minutes, I cease. That's it. I know that within hours, or a few days, the storm will come. That's the way I made the powerful Phoenix storms. Later on I discovered that the SI's had given me, without my knowing it, a long, long vocabulary of symbols to use - sent into my mind's eye, and then picked up and acted upon by them. How do they talk to me? It comes to me like a streak of lightning. In an instant, I receive a complete, complicated answer to write of my contacts, composed of perhaps three or four predictions, with details. If you have ever had an idea, or any inspirational thought come to you, that's how it is. One moment you are working at something mundane - the next moment you have received all the SI's information, the message. In the beginning, of course, I had to test it to make sure it was not just imagination. After 180 major predictions had come to pass, concerning earthquakes, hurricanes, etc., - I knew for sure that it was not imaginattion.

People ask, "How do you tell the difference between SI messages and your own thoughts, or imagination?"

Well, I know just as surely as I can look through my eyes and tell whether it is light or dark - or if what I am feeling with my fingers is soft or hard. I can easily tell the difference. And of course, after you have experienced the action and the feeling several times, it becomes familiar to you.

Now, in 1965, after I discovered it was actually UFOs that I was dealing with, and not Nature, the UFOs gave me a system to use to call upon them, just as if I'd pick up a phone and talk. They showed me, in my mind's eye, a small chamber. Inside the chamber were two small creatures, resembling grasshoppers, and insect like, but standing on two legs. These creatures looked down into a large, round oval machine. In it they could see me. If I talked, they heard the sound, but the machine quickly turned the sound into symbols, then the symbols into very high-frequency sound which they could understand.

Thus, I would talk to them in English, which would jump around into odd symbols on the screen, then result in a high whistling sound, which they understood. After talking with them for months in this manner, they suddenly, one day, pointed to a wall, upon which was a screen. They made me know that their "boss", or Higher Intelligence, would appear on this screen, and for very important communications I was to appear on the round screen and ask for "Control", and their Higher Intelligence would appear and listen to me.

And this is what happened. It wasn't a face that appeared in the screen on the wall, but a shadow which had the form of a face. The only thing to be seen clearly were two green eyes, shining from the screen. They made me know that their Higher Intelligence is made up of what we call light. No form at all. But it had made a "face" out of shadow on the screen to converse with me, because that's what I am used to talking to - a human face.

To sum up: No matter where I am or what I am doing, I can reach the SI's instantly by calling up this mental picture of the craft or chamber with the two beings in it, and seeing my face appear on the round machine, then mentally see myself telling the SI's what is needed, or what is going on. They have made a signal for me. When I request something to happen, they flash a bright light inside the chamber once for "yes" and twice for "no". "Yes" means that they will bring it about. Two flashes, or "no", means either that they cannot do it, or will not. And as their intelligence is based upon an infinite source, rather than our limited source, I humbly bow to their decisions.

They can see ahead in time, for instance. They contacted me one day and told me to warn the U.S. that the North Vietnamese would attack our carriers in Viet Nam within a few days. I called the CIA immediately and reported it. Two days later the North Vietnamese struck in a sneak attack with torpedo boats against our carriers, which were waiting for them and blew them out of the water. This is one of my 180 cases.

Their time is different from ours, and this is the main thing that presents the SI's with difficulty. They operate through what they call "time windows", producing physical effects upon our world, from their world. Their world, they tell me, is another dimension. They can produce effects from their dimension which take action and produce physical effects in our dimension.

When they simply vanish from a radar screen, instead of moving off the screen, as they have often done, they have switched to their own dimension, just like you would switch on a light. When they are ready to visit us again, they switch back to our dimension, and appear again on the radar screen, as they have also done.

But let's get back to communications. In the beginning they gave me a "vocabulary" of mental symbols to use. For instance, I would see in my mind's eye a white box labeled "Fire PK", observe the box open, see the fireballs come out of it, and see these strange symbols float across the map of the U.S. to the West Coast - and in the papers, within a few days, or a few weeks, there would come strange-looking things which would float across the map in my mind past Florida and out into the water, where I understood they were planted, like seeds. Then the seeds grew, and the hurricanes came forth. From 1963 to 1965, that's how it was - different mental symbols producing different effects.

Then in 1965 it changed. When I discovered the "chamber" method all I had to do to get results was to draw a "PK map" filled with symbols and show it on the oval machine. Then I learned to talk on the machine, and skipped the PK maps. Then they had me show them news clippings on the oval machine, from my eyes to my mind to their machine. Funny thing was - it almost always worked. That is, things happened later as a result of it, 88% of the time. The other 12% of the time it didn't, the SI's blamed on their "time-windows".

So, you say, dear readers, "Well that's fine... but how do I go about communicating with flying saucers?"

Reading how I have done it, you can imitate the method. That puts you way ahead of the game.

The SI's have told me that they put me up to this: giving out my secrets, which up to this time have been disclosed to no other human. For they wish to try to communicate with other humans besides myself. They have even constructed, in their own way, a sort of ESP channel or frequency by which this can be done by persons using my "chamber" method, with Tweeter and Twitter (my nicknames for the two strange insect-like creatures inside) in the chamber looking into the oval machine.

One thing to beware of: make sure you are willing to pay the price for contacting SI's. For instance, if I suddenly gave you a million dollars, you would probably destroy yourself in one way or another in jig time. Buy an expensive car, and crash it. Drink yourself to death, etc. Money is power, and you'd have too much power. It is the same with this. If you succeed in contacting the SI's, and some of you will (since that is the SI's wish), then they will contact you. Since this communication is all done through the medium of whatever it is, is going to have to be handled by the power of your own mind. They have told me I am the first human since the days of Moses to be able to withstand the reception of their mental sending power, or whatever it is. They have found other humans who were peculiarly adapted toward SI reception, through the years, but when they beamed or projected or whatever it is they do, the humans either cracked up completely or had strokes or cerebral hemorrhages that destroyed them.

The scientist, Zakow, mentioned earlier in this book, told me that he could understand why I had managed to withstand the awesome power-intelligence of the SI's, when they loaded my brain with it, and why others through the long years had failed to receive it and survive:

(1) For years I studied Roth's memory system. You can get the book yourself at a book store. And I practiced memorizing lists of things, using mental associations, or pictures in my mind that, in an hour, I could memorize an entire magazine. I actually gave night club and stage performances, doing this. But what it was doing was making a mental muscle - that that when SI's finally got through to me, I could handle their type of mental power, because of my years of practicing these unusual mental gymnastics.

(2) I am a master of auto-hypnosis. As a matter of fact, I used to teach this technique to other people. I specialized in it. And throughout the years, as I taught others how to hypnotize themselves, I was also deepening my own state of auto-hypnosis, so that it got so deep on my part that the SI's could tune in to me. Zakow said he did not believe the SI's could have reached me mentally without my deep experience and knowledge of self-hypnosis.

Therefore: Learn the Roth system of memory, if you can - even 20 code words, and practice them until you are automatic with them. Then get the book, "Autoconditioning", by Dr. Hornell Hart, and see what you can do about learning a bit of self-hypnosis. It is very easy to learn. Almost everyone can learn it. Thus the memory training and auto-hypnosis will increase your chance of success in reaching and working with the SI's.

This is the right way to see a flying saucer, and perhaps meet one. Do what I have told you, practicing the simple memory stunts, and learning self-hypnosis. Then, with your eyes closed, visualize a room, or chamber, with the two insect-like creatures standing over a round instrument like a kettle drum, but with a glass lens on top. Next visualize your own face peering up out of that glass lens (in effect, you are looking over the shoulders of the creatures); or looking from the side of them. Then think the words you want to tell them, and while you think the words see your mouth on the lens shaping the words you are thinking. That is as far as I can take you. That is what the SI's have told me to tell you.

If you want to try to meet their craft, go through the above and tell them you will go out into the country the next day, or in two days, etc. Then go out into the country, preferably after dark, to an area where there are no people and where you definitely won't be interrupted. Switch on a strong flashlight, set it down upon the ground, with its beam up into the air, and sit down in the dark.

If a UFO ever does come to you, force yourself to sit still. Put your hands out, palms outward, on the ground by your side, or in your lap. As it comes close, or as the intelligences get close, you may want to scream, and a sort of force or pressure may make you want to run run run. But if you can stick it out, you'll meet the SI's. I went through that ordeal one time, and will never forget it as long as I live. My hair stood up on my head; I could hardly get my breath; It was ghastly!

But wouldn't it be worth it - to meet a SI ?

BOOK TWO :

NEW INFORMATION ABOUT UFO CREATURES

INTRODUCTION

by Hurley Pennington Galbraith

In the summer 1967 issue of Saucer News appeared in print a letter to the Editor, Mr. Jim Moseley, stating that the sender, Ted Owens, would communicate with UFO intelligences and ask them to bring about a massive power blackout on the East Coast, to focus the attention of the U.S. on the upcoming Flying Saucer Convention in New York.

JUST A FEW WEEKS LATER AFTER THE LETTER APPEARED IN THE SAUCER NEWS, CAME THE GREAT DAYTIME BLACKOUT OF JUNE 5, 1967!

Murray Zatman, Esq., lawyer with one of the top law firms of Philadelphia was informed by Ted Owens that the June 5 blackout would be forthcoming before June 21, and when the blackout did in fact occur, Mr. Zatman confirmed that Owens had predicted the SI's (space intelligences) would cause it.

Owens informed Zatman that the SI's would cause a hurricane to occur within a week's time, the first hurricane of 1967 - and predicted it would come up the East Coast. When the hurricane appeared within five days, and did come up the East coast, Zatman confirmed same.

The Philadelphia Evening Bulletin confirmed, in a long article, that Owens had written in to its Editor, well in advance, of numerous rainstorms during the drought, predicting that he would make the storms happen, and that the storms arrived when Owens said they would.

Ted Owens

Owens told the radio audience on the Jack McKinney "Night Talk" show, in 1966, that he would cause UFOs to come to the Philadelphia area from all over the world. In 1967 a magazine article appeared (National Enquirer) stating that the scientific world was baffled because of the thousands of UFO sightings in the state of Pennsylvania that had occurred - more than anywhere else.

Owens told Tim Beckley (Editor of Searchlight) that he would ask the UFOs to produce three simultaneous hurricanes during the year of 1967, so rare that it had only happened five times in history! The three simultaneous hurricanes did then appear.

Owens told Roland Swank, scientist with Systems Management Analysis, Philadelphia, that he would ask the UFOs to make Hurricane Inez turn right to Cuba, go to the tip of Florida, stop, then reverse itself and take Hurricane Betsy's path of the year before. Inez went to Cuba, turned right, stopped at the tip of Florida, backed up, and took Betsy's path of the year before, just as Owens predicted.

Owens told Jack McKinney (Night Talk Radio Show) and Ed Harvey (Talk of Philadelphia Radio Show) over the air, that even though the United States was in a six-year drought, he would ask the SI's to end the drought. After these broadcasts came the rains - the great East Coast drought ended.

Owens then went on the same radio stations and announced that, to prove this was no accident, he would ask the UFO intelligences to end the killer-drought in India, which the experts said would kill four million persons in 1967. After the broadcasts, the rains came to India, and the Indian Government announced the drought was over and the four million people would be fed and would not die.

In 1965 Owens saved the life of a girl with a crushed skull in a Washington, D.C., hospital, by using the UFO Intelligences' power. The girl's name was Brenda Sue Pennington, given up for dead by the doctors before Owens received permission to use SI power on her. She is now alive and lives in Rainelle, West Virginia.

This could go on and on - for Owens has 181 documented cases of these miracles that he has caused, by communicating with Saucer Intelligences and requesting that they bring them about.

But another book must be written about them, and will come later. This book is being written because Owens met, by accident, a teenager named Chuck Jay, introduced to him by a prominent writer. The boy asked permission to come to the home of Owens, and question him about the SI's, and what he knew of the UFOs. Owens agreed. Chuck proved to be such a brilliant questioner, in spite of his young age, that Owens decided to put the taped session into book form, so that people all over the world who are interested in UFO phenomena might have a greater insight and knowledge into how the UFO intelligences think, feel and operate.

This, then, is that book. Read on, and know that all that is written herein is absolutely true, as stated by Ted Owens (President of the Sotas, Box 170005, Philadelphia, Pa. 19105) to the best of his knowledge, and his 181 documented cases, many of which are confirmed and notarized by responsible persons such as lawyers, notaries, police, etc.

Now, meet the SI's!

- H.P.G., January, 1969

Ted Owens

QUESTIONS and ANSWERS

QUESTIONS: CHUCK JAY

ANSWERS: TED OWENS President, The Sotas

Q. Have the SI's been among us on the earth?

A. Yes, the SI's been among us on the earth.

Q. You say they like children... and they work with children... what kind of work are they doing?

A. If you were going to sow a crop, as a farmer, what would you take out in the fields to plant - half-grown corn cobs?

Q. I would take what I wanted to grow.

A. Yes, you would take seeds. Children are seeds. If the U.S. can survive for the next year or two, the children that have grown up by that time, and which the SI's have reached, will be important to the SI's, in their work with humans on earth. Now, I'll give you a beautiful illustration of this. Yesterday afternoon I came home from work, fell into my chair, hot and tired, took off my shoes, and the downstairs door-buzzer buzzed. I put on my shoes and went downstairs, and there was a long-distance phone call for me from New Jersey.

It was a 13-year-old boy who had heard me over a local radio program in 1965, two years ago, and he had been trying to find me ever since. That boy was brilliant, absolutely brilliant. He asked me questions that were a lot better than any questions that have been asked of me on any of the many radio and TV interview programs I have been on. This boy said he had an old box full of UFO material in his home, everything he could lay his hands on which dealt with UFOs. He said that he and his mother and father had been in their car, driving on the New Jersey Turnpike one evening when suddenly they saw a flying saucer right over them. They pulled to the side of the road, and the UFO was 50 feet directly over them. Ever since that day he has been doing nothing but thinking about and studying about UFOs. Do you see what I mean about their working with children?

Q. So they are making the children interested in them?

A. You bet they are! They are establishing a contact with them. But the problem is, they can contact the minds of children but the children cannot communicate back with the SI's. It is not a two-way proposition. That is where I come in. I have written a book, giving my exact method of communicating with the SI's. Complete. This is for the purpose of children being able to get in touch with the SI's.

Q. Do the SI's have any influence on the "prophets" of our day?

A. Prophets? Yes, a great deal of influence. Of course, you have to bear in mind that SI's monitor the thinking of our key people in high places, as well as other people in low places that we would not suspect they would be interested in - and they influence their thinking, certainly they do. They also influence the masses of people through television.

Q. The "prophets" don't know of this, do they? I mean, they don't know their thinking is being influenced.

A. That's right - they don't know it - they think their thoughts and predictions are their own; but in many cases they are simply reflecting what the SI's are putting into their minds.

Q. Then the SI's are having the "prophets" do certain work?

A. Yes. You see, the SI's are interested in the entire human race as a whole - not the black race, the white race, the yellow race, etc., as such. They aren't interested in our race problems, or our politics. They are interested only in making the surface of the world healthy and happy and productive, growing and creative. So they influence key people toward certain things, like chess pieces on a board, and these people do not realize they are being manipulated, but they are, according to the SI's wishes - to bring about results among the masses of people.

The SI's even bring about revolutions. Israel is a case in point. You see, Israel is a small, tough, virile country. The people are very virile, full of energy, full of action. The Arabs and Egyptians have become very lazy through the ages, and sloppy, and they let the land go, to a greater extent. But the Israelis take a small piece of land and through hard work make the land fertile and productive. This is what the SI's want. They want the desert to bloom, and become productive. They are interested primarily in the healthy condition of the surface of the earth, and all that lives on that surface.

Q. Is it possible that we can ever reach the SI's level of intelligence? You know, like being able to move things with our minds, and so forth.

A. Absolutely impossible. They have different powers than we. They have different laws of nature. You see, the SI's are in a different world entirely. They are in another dimension. But they have discovered how to switch from their dimension into our dimension. Thus they have access both to their world and our world, while we are limited to our world. So we could never do what the SI's can do.

Q. In other words, we are completely different, then, from the SI's.

A. Yes, completely different.

Q. Is there a wall between our dimension and their dimension? Couldn't we, some way, get into their dimension?

A. We don't know how to do this, but they do know how. Just suppose, for a moment, we were SI's. We could make ourselves invisible, then appear right out in a field, or inside Cape Kennedy, or inside a crowded city - in the earth dimension. We would see these strange creatures (humans, us), yet the strange creatures (humans, us) couldn't see us (SI's) unless we wanted them to, at which time we could make ourselves visible, or in some form we wanted to made visible. But if we remained invisible then we could observe the earth creatures at their work and at their play.

Q. You mean, then, that there could be a SI or SI's right here, right now, watching us?

A. Absolutely. Now suppose we, as SI's, switch ourselves into this other dimension, this earth dimension, to observe these earth creatures performing all sorts of actions - and we wish to experiment with these earth creatures, to get some results with them. We can do one of two things: we can go into the earth dimension, and work with the earth creatures, unbeknownst to them, or we can switch ourselves back into our own SI world, or dimension, we can cause ship wrecks and plane wrecks or submarine wrecks in the earth world, or dimension. In other words, we, as SI's while in the SI world, or dimension, can produce effects across other worlds or dimensions.

Or what would you do if a man, seemingly on dope, walked up to you and pulled out a long butcher knife and said he was going to kill you? All of these things happened to me, and I'll tell you what I did. For instance, I was with my girl-friend, Pat, one night in Durham, North Carolina, when we were both attending Duke University. We had gone downtown together, and were walking up a dark side street, when a gang of six toughs came at us. As they got closer, I could see they had knives. I recognized their leader as the man who had tried to climb through a window of Pat's home a few nights before. I had chased him down the street when Pat's mother screamed. Now they had us cornered on this small side street, and expected us to run from them. I had a small .25 automatic, and gave it to Pat and told her if any of them got past to shoot them. Then I walked right down the street at the gang toward us. I stared them all in the eyes, and they froze. I grabbed the ring-leader by his coat and told him to take his gang and get away from us. And that is just what they did. The following week the same gang of men killed a North Carolina college student, and they all went to prison.

Another time in Durham, while I was in college, I took a date to a beautiful park. We were walking along when about 15 boys in their late teens circled us with bicycles and shouted obscene language at us. I stood in the center of their circle and begged them to come fight me one at a time, as many as wanted to, or all; it didn't make any difference to me - and they froze. All of them stopped their bikes, and there was complete silence. Then suddenly they took off as fast as they could go, without saying another word. Again, in Durham, I was escorting two foreign girl students through the town one night, and three notoriously tough men came at me, and began talking obscenely to the girls. I stared at them, told them to shut up and move off, and they froze, then moved away silently. People nearby couldn't believe their eyes, because these three men were never known to have left their victims without cutting them up or beating them severely. Later, in Oklahoma, a New York gangster with a reputation as a killer got into an argument with me, and pulled out a .45 automatic, aimed it at me, and was going to shoot me. I looked into his eyes, and he froze. I just turned my back, walked away, and left him standing there, silent. Another time, in Houston, Texas, a car with four men in it pulled up to me and pointed guns at me. They ordered me to get into the car. To this day I don't know who they were, or why they wanted me; but I walked over to their car, right at the gun muzzles; looked at each of the men, and they froze. Then I silently turned and walked away.

Q. Were the SI's protecting you?

A. I guess so. Yes.

Q. Since you are part SI now?

A. Right. And this sort of thing has gone on through the years. I should have been killed about 15 times by now. Another exciting incident occurred when a blonde woman hired me to drive her down to Mexico City. She paid me a thousand dollars, told me she was running away from her cruel husband. What she didn't tell me, until we were halfway there, was that she had stolen all the money out of their joint bank account, sold their home and business, and had the divorce papers served on her husband - the very day we left for Mexico City! How she must have hated him. Anyway, I got her down to Mexico City safely, and started back to the States. At the edge of Durango I stopped for gas at a filling station. A small boy was the attendant. I went into the station office to pay the boy, when suddenly two men came to the door. One stood just outside the door, keeping watch, and the other came in, pulling a knife from his pocket. The boy was petrified, and told me these were very bad men, that he knew them. Instantly I realized the blonde had decided to buy some insurance that I wouldn't give her hiding place away to her husband, and had sent these men after me. I stared the knife-man in the eyes, and he froze. I walked to the door and stared the other man in the eyes, then walked by him, got to my car, and drove out of there as fast as I could. But just before I got to San Antonio, still in Mexico, a truck with two men in it rammed me from behind at full speed, whip lashing me violently and knocking me out. When I came to, on the ground outside my car where I'd been thrown by the impact, the truck was still parked behind my car and the men were in it. I got up, went up to them, stared them in the eyes, and they drove off without saying a word. Another time, my daughter Lornie and I were walking along a sidewalk in San Antonio, when suddenly a man crossed the street, walked toward me, pulled out a long knife, and said over and over that he was going to kill me. I put down my satchel (I was selling Bibles) and put Lornie behind me. As the man approached, I looked him in the eyes. He came up to within a few feet of me, had the knife on his right hip, professional style, with cutting edge up. I stared into his eyes. Suddenly he dropped the knife, got down on his knees, and began to pat Lornie on the head (she had edged around to see what was going on). He apologized to Lornie for threatening me, picked up his knife, and ran away.

Q. Do you think that all of these strange occurrences, these threats to you, might have been because of the evil SI's - the Oi's.

A. That might be so. I will tell you this: there was a brilliant scientist up here one night to see me. He has three doctoral degrees, including one in astro-physics. I proposed and experiment to him. I pointed my fingers at his eyes, the way I do at the sky when I am "making" a storm, and asked him if he could feel anything peculiar. You have never seen a man recoil so fast in your life! He jumped up to his feet, looked away from my pointing fingers, and turned absolutely white! My fingers pointed at him seemed to scare the living daylights out of him! It's funny, I don't know why I did that at all - the idea just occurred to me to see how it might affect his eyes, or his mind. I also told this scientist about a "grid" that I had put over the Florida area, in my mind, the way the SI's had taught me - a grid composed of four sliding bars of different colors, which the SI's had given to me to understand would create an electromagnetic area over Cape Kennedy. To me, this grid, although I had made it, and used it, had never meant anything other than some symbol of the SI's. I had even made a crayon picture of it, but didn't know what, if anything, it meant. But to the scientist, this was the most exciting thing I had shown him! He said, "Wait a minute! That's the best thing you have told me yet! Did you know that is a regular scientific piece of apparatus?" I said no, I don't know. He said, "Why, they have those in scientific laboratories, those grids." As I remember it and understand it, he explained that only my "frequency" could get through the grid - or perhaps it was only the SI's frequency that could get through the grid to Cape Kennedy. Anyway, that was the general idea.

Q. Are these things down there protecting Cape Kennedy?

A. Not protecting it - attacking it!

Q. You said you have made crayon drawings of some of the SI things. Could I see them?

A. Certainly. Here they area. This one shows four great SI craft, positioned around our globe. For want of a better name I call them the "Emmy-Emma" group (a nickname for them given by my son, Rick). It is these four craft I signal when I wish to give a demonstration of earthquakes all over the world, as I have done twice, for government agencies and scientists. These craft are so big, we couldn't even imagine their size. Each one could be bigger than our earth itself.

Q. Why can't we seem them, then?

A. They are in another dimension. Now, I have proved the reality of them, because several times I have signaled them (first writing to the scientists and government agencies what I was going to do) and after I signaled them, they issued an electromagnetic effect which affected the rate of the earth's spin or movement a trifle, causing earthquakes, floods and dramatically unusual weather. First I wrote and told what I was going to do - and then it actually happened. In the days and weeks following my signal to these four craft, there were tremendous floods, earthquakes, tornados and hurricanes all over the world! I have put all the clippings from newspapers of all these happenings with the letter I sent to the scientists and government agencies, as proof. I have done this twice, and each time it has worked. It has not failed yet.

Q. I believe you said that about 200 of these experiments you have conducted have come true; isn't that right?

A. Yes, I have just successfully finished my 181st documented experiment with SI's.

Q. What is this crayon drawing?

A. This is how the SI's affect people when they are over an area. They fly over an area in their craft, and Twitter and Tweeter (my nickname for these humanoid forms with grasshopper heads, remember) act out their thoughts on a machine... and broadcast these thoughts to the people below... maybe through the TV sets in the peoples' homes below, I'm not sure... however, in this way they can and do affect the minds of masses of people.

Q. And what is this crayon picture?

A. This is the "master control" I was telling you about - the higher SI Intelligence which Twitter and Tweeter contact on the wall of their craft. Control appears on a TV-like screen, a blurred outline of a human face, full-on, and all you can really make out clearly are the eyes. The SI's told me that I am able to see a face for Control because I am used to talking to human faces - so that is what they gave me to look at, for Control, when I am talking to him. Suffice it to say, Control does not have a human face, or head.

Q. You mean they did that just so you wouldn't be talking to the wall, or to empty space, when you addressed Control?

A. That's right.

Q. And the SI's call it "Control"?

A. Yes. Now here is another picture. It shows what Twitter and Tweeter look like

(Note: This interview and taping took place in 1967. In 1968 both Saucer News and a national magazine printed a picture reputedly photographed by a Russian, in Russia, of a creature that had been thrown from a flying saucer when it crashed or burned. This creature in Russia had a humanoid body, with a head identical to that I had drawn of Twitter and Tweeter in 1965 in crayon... triangular-shaped head, huge eyes on the side of the head, and a nose coming to a point - and possibly mouth combined. And in my crude crayon drawing, Twitter and Tweeter also had humanoid bodies.)

Now this machine is what they look down into, when they see me and talk to me. They call their machine "Men-Tel", for "mental television". When I converse with them, I am looking downward, from the right of them, at their side, and see them looking downward into the Men-Tel where my face appears in the machine.

Q. That is what was done here in the apartment?

A. No, no. That is what they have taught me to contact, whenever I wish to communicate with them.

Q. How long does it take for you to make contact with them... to communicate with them?

A. In a fraction of a second - instantly. As quickly as it would take you to put a picture-slide into a projector, to project it onto a viewing screen. Whenever I want to be with the SI's to communicate, like a snap of my fingers, I am there. Then if I want to go higher up, for something very special or important, I ask them to call Control. I say "This is very important... may I see Control?" Then the shadowy face appears on the empty frame on the wall, and I talk to it. It has life; it moves; the eyes are alive.

Q. These symbols ...are they what you use to communicate with?

A. No. And let me tell you about that, because it's a very weird thing, how it all happened. I first made that crayon drawing because the SI's told me that when I come on the Men-Tel and speak English, it is then translated into these strange looking symbols, which are then further translated into sound - a sort of high frequency squeaking-whistling sound which they can understand. Well, long after I drew these crayon drawings, I ran across this picture of symbols in a copy of Fate Magazine. As you can see, they are the very same symbols I had drawn long before, which, a Florida farmer had found after a spacecraft had been near him. Immediately, when I saw the symbols on the page of Fate magazine I ran and got my records and dug out my crayon drawings - and the symbols of my drawing, and the symbols on that paper in Fate... were identical! See, compare them!

Q. And you made this crayon drawing a long time before you found this picture in Fate magazine?

A. Yes, a long time before. Over a year before.

Q. How fascinating. What is this crayon picture of?

A. This is a picture of the monitor they use on me whenever I go. It is like a beam of light which extends from me through metal or rock or any material, high up into the sky, high up into the atmosphere, wherever I happen to be: in a deep cave underground or on top of a skyscraper.

Q. And they know what you are thinking, by this monitor device?

A. That's right. No matter where I am, they know what is happening to me: where I am, what I am thinking, what I am feeling, what my eyes see, and so on.

Q. What is this crayon drawing of a human head?

A. This picture shows how they have actually changed my brain. They communicated with me one day, and told me to make a colored picture of this. Somehow, in time gone by, they have changed the right lobe of my brain, so that I could get to this point with them - because the ordinary human brain will not pick up or send back intelligence to the SI's. Also the ordinary human brain will break down under SI communication. That is why I am so rare, according to them. Through the ages, since the time of Moses (they were able to do with Moses what they have done with me), they have attempted to build up other humans they would communicate with and work with; but the humans always had a heart attack or brain hemorrhage or broke down completely in some way.

Q. Why didn't they stop, when they saw that the person they were trying to work with was going to have a heart attack or stroke, or whatever?

A. I don't believe they could do anything about it. In other words, when the SI's would exert their force of intelligence to the potential human receiver they had selected, the receiver would break down. Just as we might put too much electricity in some mechanical device, which would be destroyed by the overload, or break down.

Q. If they can affect the minds of masses of people, how come those human minds don't break down, or die?

A. Because there is a great difference. When they send intelligence to the humans en masse... the intelligence goes through those human minds like an x-ray. But when they wish a human to catch their intelligence, and communicate back, then the human must retain his power, be able to catch their power, instead of letting it go on through their brain - and it is the retention of SI power which is too much for the human brain.

Q. Then once they start sending intelligence to the receiver, human, it acts just like a chain-reaction that destroys the human brain?

A. I never thought of it that way, but I suppose that pretty well sums it up.

Q. How come you didn't die, then?

A. With me, it "took". It's difficult for me to explain it, but I'll try. Through the years past, I should have been killed about 15 times. When I was five, a car knocked me into the air and threw me thirty feet. I was out like a light for seven hours, then woke up and went about my business as if it had never happened.

When I was three years old I picked up and ate enough strychnine, hidden in coconut candy and put in our front yard, to kill three grown men. But my mother saw the candy in my mouth, ran me next door to a doctor, who pumped out my stomach and identified the poison. I rolled down the bank into a river, when my mother took me to a picnic when I was about a year old, and floated away downstream. It was very peaceful, and I can still remember looking up and seeing the sunlight on the top of the water over my head. Luckily, Bus Doub, a boy at the picnic, saw me, dove in, and pulled me out. I had held my breath all that time and didn't inhale any water at all. This sort of thing went on all through my life. Now, the SI's can get into your mind - when you're asleep, or unconscious through an injury. And this they did. They knew I was "different" from the ordinary human, since I became a hypnotist when I was 13, an expert on voodoo and juju when I was 10, and so forth. I mastered more than 20 professions through the years - not as a jack-of-all-trades, but I mastered these professions. So the SI's knew they had a flexible mind to work with, that could master any profession it sought out. They knew I had a strong mind, for some of that professional work involved judo training and bodyguard work that required my mettle to be tested rather severely. And I mastered auto-hypnosis and used it extensively. So they knew that this, an integral function of working with the SI's, fitted into the Owens jig-saw puzzle. Then I developed tremendous ESP powers, worked with Dr. Rhine at the Duke Parapsychology Lab; and thus further enhanced my possibilities with the SI's. Finally, by putting some adventurous ideas into my head, they "talked" me into taking long trips through isolated areas. It was then that they reached me physically (I lost all track of time on those trips. I would think it was Wednesday, and it would turn out to be Thursday or Friday), and some real miracles happened on those trips. But it was then that the SI's were able to come down and do something, using their own techniques and powers, to my brain, in order to better enable me to communicate with them, and survive their communicating power.

They have been able to keep me alive, and survive all I've been through... which ordinarily I could not possibly have survived.

Q. And that picture is your PK system?

A. Yes.

Q. With that, you can move objects with your mind?

A. Yes, I have moved objects with my mind. While at Duke University years ago, Dr. Rhine requested I give a private demonstration of my ESP powers for himself, his wife, Louisa, and several other scientists. Dr. Rhine set up the experiment in his living room. My "assignment" was to sit ten feet away from a table, on which he had propped up securely a pair of heavy scissors, and knock the scissors down with my mind power. For an hour I labored mentally, to knock the scissors down. Then just as I was about to give up and say to heck with it, the scissors flew off the table with a loud "whack" noise, and landed some four or five feet away. They had not fallen down - they had been knocked clear off the table. The scientists were stunned. And actually, so was I. It's impossible to ever get used to defying what to us are the laws of nature. Another time, while with my family in Los Angeles, I was changing a tire on my car, which was parked on a steep downhill angle, in close to the curb. The car slipped off the jack onto my hand, crushing my hand into the sharp angle of the corner of the curb and the car. Since many of my professions depend on two good hands - judo, painting, photography, drumming, typing, and so on - instantly I could not stand the thought of that hand being crushed. It seemed as if time stood still, and I "willed" that my hand be released. (I didn't stop to figure this out, or reason. There was no time for it; it just happened.) Believe it or not, the car rose into the air by itself. I jerked my hand away, and the car fell back down with a crash! Although my hand was aching and had a deep crease on the back of it, all I could do was stand there in a fog, realizing I had just witnessed a miracle. Then I examined my hand. Nothing broken, nothing hurt at all. It should have been mangled, ground to a pulp, smashed. This was repeated at a later date, in a different way. An airplane mechanic was repairing my car on his day off, in the front yard of his home in Biloxi, Mississippi. He had the hood up, and was inspecting the back of the car radiator. He said, "Ted, I've found the leak in the radiator". I said, "Where?" and without looking just stuck my arm around the corner of the car... straight into the fan of the car (the motor was running). The mechanic stared at me in horror, and his face turned white. As soon as my hand and wrist went into the spinning fan, I realized my error. There was a loud whacking sound, and I took my hand out. The mechanic cried, "My god! Isn't it hurt?" I shook my head. There wasn't a mark on my hand or wrist. The mechanic said, "That's impossible!" And it was. But in this case it happened before I thought, unlike the other two cases.

Q. Here is another picture. Will you explain it?

A. Yes, this is a picture of how the SI's influence the minds of masses of people through TV sets. They can broadcast from their space ship, and it comes through your TV set into your mind, on a subliminal level, while you are watching "Gunsmoke", for instance. Incidentally, the SI's have told me that they gave us humans the idea of TV, just for this purpose, so that they could broadcast thoughts and ideas to humans through the TV sets.

Q. How about radio?

A. I don't know about radio.

Q. And this picture?

A. This is a picture of the PK area which extends from Jacksonville, Florida, down to Miami, Florida, that I talked about before - the area known as "Electro". This area is growing in PK power all the time.

Q. Is this a physical thing?

A. No, it's in another dimension, affecting that particular area, and it is growing right there and having a constant effect right there. To get the idea, think of a photo negative being held over a picture print, with the superimposed negative having an effect on the print, cumulatively, increasing as times goes by. Here, you see, is the "grid" I talked about earlier. This PK area, and the grid, is what killed the 3 astronauts some time ago in that tragedy at Cape Kennedy, because the SI's were angry with the U.S. Government at the time.

Q. It wasn't the oxygen in the capsule?

A. No. Let me tell you something: lightning hit a lightning-proof pad down there at Cape Kennedy, AFTER I wrote a letter to NASA and said it would happen. And when I went to Washington and talked to Mr. Eastwood, of NASA, he said this single occurrence had puzzled them at NASA the most: how lightning could strike an especially prepared pad. It was supposed to be impossible. Since then it has happened several times.

Q. What is this picture, of lightning coming out of your hand?

A. The SI's told me, when I first began this work, to "see" in my mind lightning coming out of my hand, which I pointed at the sky, whenever I wanted to make a storm. Then they would take over and make the storm. They understood the symbol- signal. In effect, the SI's taught me how to use a mental-imagery vocabulary which they could understand, and take action on.

Q. You are like a spark-plug to get an experiment started, after that they take over and bring it about?

A. Exactly. A little spark can set off a tremendous explosion.

Q. Well, this has changed my thinking of UFO's, you know. Changed it completely.

A. It has changed my thinking, too.

Q. Just recently a lot of UFO's were seen down in Florida by some school kids and their teachers. Did you read about that?

A. That was my doing, believe it or not. Not long ago at my office a group of people who know of my work got together and asked me to contact the SI's and have them do something for a demonstration. Ordinarily I don't like that request; they resent it, in fact, because SI's aren't a night club act or a circus. So I started to politely refuse, but the SI's cut in instantly and told me to go ahead. So I told the group I would ask the SI's to make a great big dramatic appearance that would be written up in the newspapers. And they certainly did! This group of people gave me a signed, notarized confirmation of the experiment.

Q. Why do the SI's want to help us, as you say they do?

A. I don't know. I haven't the foggiest notion of why. I have wondered about that myself. But the SI's say they helped Moses, so you could ask yourself, "Why they would help Moses?" Why would they help a man who was tending sheep, and to his business, take off and go clear to Egypt to butt heads with the great Pharaoh and the entire Egyptian army? Why would they do that?

Q. Would Russia and China be willing to let the SI's make a base in their country, in order to spread peace around the world.

A. I don't know whether they would or not. I can't speak for those countries. However, I will say this: in my opinion Russia has a better attitude and open mind on this subject than the U.S., and I believe I would have more opportunity to arrange a meeting between the SI's and the top Russian leaders, than I have here in the U.S. I'll tell you why. They have made great progress in Russia in working with ESP. Suppose you had ESP powers in Russia. They would take you and put you in a special ESP school, or college, which exists for training people with these special abilities. The expense would be Russia's and would cost you nothing. This way they round up all the good ESP people they find, all over Russia. But in the U.S.? They laugh. There are just a few ESP laboratories, to my knowledge, in the U.S., of which, Duke is a fine one. But then, the only persons tested - not trained, tested - are those lucky students with enough money to go to college, and even those are just tested and let go on their jolly way. One boy I know clairvoyantly guessed 25 card symbols out of 25 card symbols - and what happened? He just went ahead with his ordinary college studies and left college, as if nothing had happened. This wouldn't have happened in Russia! They would have placed too high a value on that boy's ability. Just think of all the thousands of potentially good ESP people walking around in the U.S. - grocers, clerks, farmers, etc. Their ability is utterly lost to this country! However, I myself wouldn't want to live in Russia, and have to take orders. I'll take the freedom of the U.S., with all the drawbacks of the U.S., anytime.

Q. What do the other nations of the world think about the SI's? Or don't they know about them?

A. Sure. They know about them. At least that is what I read in the newspapers and magazines.

Q. What do the American people think about the SI's?

A. It was stated recently by some organization that had checked it out that over 5 million Americans have seen UFO's, at one time or another. What the people think about it, I wouldn't know.

Q. Does President Johnson know anything about the SI's?

A. He knows about the UFO's. I don't know if he knows anything about my form of SI's or not. If he has read any of the correspondence I have sent him, then he knows plenty about the SI's.

Q. How long has the U.S. Government believed in UFO's?

A. I guess since Kenneth Arnold first spotted them in Washington. Wasn't that about 1947?

Q. If the U.S. Government doesn't let the SI's help us, how many more years would you say we have to survive?

A. About three years... at the maximum. (Through 1970).

Q. Why have the SI's appeared around all of our major military installations?

A. They don't confide in me on things like that - they simply give me assignments and training, all pointing at certain objectives. Just about everything they communicate to me deals with the assignments I am working on with them. They do give me details of what is going to happen ahead - what they are going to cause to happen - so that I can write in to the scientists and agencies so there will be written proof when it occurs. But they have one great big over-all plan in mind, whatever it may be; and they are trying to complete it.

Q. Then you wouldn't know why the UFO's trailed the Gemini flights and some other flights in outer space?

A. Certainly! I wrote in to the Government and told them that the SI's were going to do that, as proof that they were real and that they can communicate with me.

Q. Why were the SI's over Washington in 1952?

A. All I can tell you is that was when I was in Washington with my family, seeing NASA and CIA about the SI's, the papers were full of UFO's doing this and doing that over the Washington area at that time. The UFO's were as thick as fleas there then.

Q. Has the Government ever asked you to give a demonstration to prove that you are in communication with the SI's?

A. Yes. When I was down in Washington talking to the CIA, they asked me to have the SI's do something right there in the room with us. You know, like make the table float in the air, and so forth. But I explained that that was not what the SI's did - not how they work. The SI's will make a hurricane back up or turn around, but they won't do parlor tricks.

Q. The SI you saw in your bedroom - had it taken on the shape of a man just for your benefit? You said the SI's could make different shapes out of themselves.

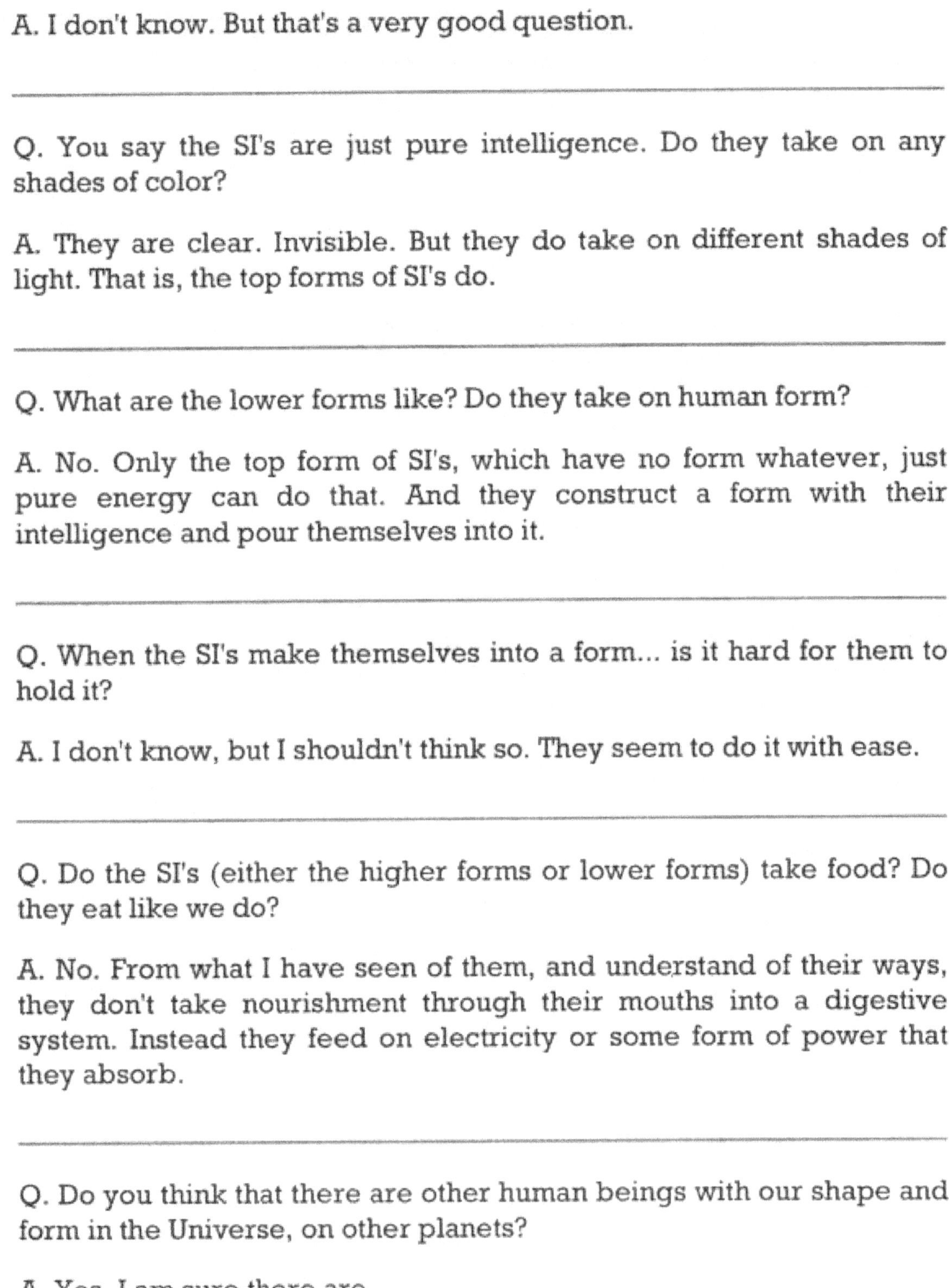

A. I don't know. But that's a very good question.

Q. You say the SI's are just pure intelligence. Do they take on any shades of color?

A. They are clear. Invisible. But they do take on different shades of light. That is, the top forms of SI's do.

Q. What are the lower forms like? Do they take on human form?

A. No. Only the top form of SI's, which have no form whatever, just pure energy can do that. And they construct a form with their intelligence and pour themselves into it.

Q. When the SI's make themselves into a form... is it hard for them to hold it?

A. I don't know, but I shouldn't think so. They seem to do it with ease.

Q. Do the SI's (either the higher forms or lower forms) take food? Do they eat like we do?

A. No. From what I have seen of them, and understand of their ways, they don't take nourishment through their mouths into a digestive system. Instead they feed on electricity or some form of power that they absorb.

Q. Do you think that there are other human beings with our shape and form in the Universe, on other planets?

A. Yes. I am sure there are.

Q. Well, many people have seen these human-like creatures getting out of flying saucers, all over the world...

A. I still say that the higher forms of SI's are taking that shape. Either that, or they can hypnotize us humans who see them into believing they have human form.

Q. Some people claim to have seen inside flying saucers... and they saw the pilots.

A. After seeing and knowing my SI's it is hard for me to believe that there are SI's with our human form.

Q. Why is it that flying saucers never seem to have accidents?

A. Well, mine never have. My SI's, from another dimension, never have accidents. It is impossible.

Q. Why don't they?

A. For the same reason they can't be destroyed. For the same reason nobody has been able to shoot them down, and it's been tried. They have other-dimensional properties. In other words, there are other powers that these SI's have which we do not even know about - laws of Nature, their Nature, you might say, on their side of their dimension which they can bring with them into our dimension.

Q. Why do flying saucers affect cars and electrical instruments when they come close?

A. I'm glad you asked that, because the SI's just recently explained it to me, since I'd been wondering about it myself. It has been commonly assumed that it is an accidental occurrence, due to some form of nuclear power which powers the craft. But here is what the SI's have told me. When they come into an area they want to investigate, they throw out a "net", just like a fisherman throws his net overboard from his boat to trap fish. They extend an electromagnetic net all around them that will trap and stop all power in that area in order to keep anybody from being able to communicate with humans outside the SI "net" - to radio for help, or radio for airplane interference, etc.

Q. Since we can't do anything to them or their craft, and as you have said, they can't be destroyed, why do they use this net?

A. They don't know everything. These SI's I know are quite different from the ones I have read about, and they have their own way of doing things. They are much wiser than we are. They must know what they are doing. Let's put it like this: why don't they want us to shoot at them. Or look at it this way: why don't the Forest Rangers who take care of our National forests, shoot bears and animals, instead of tranquilizing them and tagging them? The SI's could actually destroy all humans in their area if they wanted, instead of throwing out a tranquilizing, power-stopping electromagnetic "net".

Q. Well, when we shoot at their craft, doesn't it annoy them?

A. Right! They don't want to hurt us. That's why they use their EM net, so people won't call for help and raise a rumpus and force the SI's to leave the area, where they have planned something, or force the SI's to take action against the attacking humans. This is something the SI's don't want. However, whenever humans go at the SI's with hostile intent, they have a way of turning the thought of the hostile humans right back onto them - just like you would bounce a ball against the wall and it would bounce back again; or just like you would shine a light in the mirror, and the reflection would come right back at you. This is a power that SI's have and that we don't have. So if a flying saucer came down in an area, and somebody saw it, and called for help - and planes came to chase it and shoot at it - somebody would get hurt, and it wouldn't be the SI's. And the SI's don't want that. They are peaceful in intent, and are trying to keep things that way. After all, the reason they are here is to help us, if we will let them.

Q. These people who make predictions: do the SI's put a lot of this in their heads?

A. Yes, I am sure that they do, although the humans making the predictions do not know it, of course, I am certain that the great prophets of biblical times got their prophecy material from the SI's, since I know, personally, that the SI's teach and pass on information while a human is asleep and dreaming. And as you know, many prophets of the Bible got their information through pictures in their dreams.

Q. You say the SI's teach humans in their sleep? How is that?

A. They switch themselves from their dimension into this dimension right into your room. You can't see them, ordinarily, but we have seen them in our apartment, unexpectedly. Our doors and windows were closed and locked, with no way for them to get in. I can tell you, absolutely and positively, that they have talked to me and trained me in my sleep, night after night after night. I could tell you about that, but it would be too lengthy and complicated to go into here. One interesting thing, though: I woke up one night, about 4 in the morning, and a voice was speaking from deep down inside my throat. My mouth was closed tight, my eyes were open, and this voice was speaking from inside my throat - not using my speech muscles at all!

Q. Do you believe that we are going to have germ warfare with China, like Jean Dixon has predicted?

A. Jean Dixon? Why, I have predicted that myself! To my contacts. Sure, don't look for a nuclear war, first. Look for germ and bacteriological attacks! I didn't know Dixon predicted that too. How interesting. Well, I think Russia and China will attack us, both at the same time. Then if that method doesn't destroy us, they will use the nuclear method.

Q. Can prayers help us in our situation?

A. Prayers can help you in any situation. But don't forget, the millions of Jews who were butchered by the Nazis in the last war, probably prayed too, but it didn't stop them from getting butchered. But the SI's, who are closer to God and spiritual power than we are, have tremendous powers that can save us, if we let them. Remember that the SI's are intelligences, not human creatures that can be destroyed, but intelligences which cannot be destroyed. But you bet, prayer will help anyone. I could tell you a couple of times in my life when nothing human could help me, I prayed, and miracles happened!

Q. How many planets are there in the solar system?

A. What? Planets? I wouldn't know about that. I've never discussed anything like that with the SI's.

Q. I have read that some scientists believe other worlds have come close to our earth, but we can't see those worlds, They are invisible to us, sort of like your "other dimension".

A. I haven't seen those articles, but it certainly would fit into what I've found out. Yes.

Q. Do the SI's have anything to do with the comets coming close to earth?

A. I don't know that. But I can tell you that a lot of so-called "comets" seen from earth, are not comets. They are SI craft. Not long ago the SI's communicated with me, and told me they were going to come over Philadelphia in their craft, as a sign to me and to our government that they are real, and are in communication with me. I notified the scientists and government agencies of this, and went out and bought a camera, to take a picture of it when it came over. Just six days later the now famous "East Coast Fireball" came over Philadelphia, written up in Life Magazine, but called by some astronomers a "comet". But the SI's had told me to expect them to come over Philadelphia, and they did so. It was certainly "comet". I had called it six days in advance, as a SI craft.

Q. Then many of the so-called "comets" are really great big SI craft, or flying saucers, with SI's in them?

A. Yes, that's right.

Q. How do they manufacture their craft? In factories? Those you say are as large as our earth - how do they make flying saucers that big?

A. They don't make or manufacture material things like we do. They don't use machine tools, or factories, that is, from what I know of them. It's done by their mental power, or intelligence.

Q. If they can move objects with their minds, or intelligence then I suppose they can form these craft by use of their strange intelligence powers?

A. Yes. I am sure that they don't put them together with nuts and bolts.

Q. Why are plants being collected by space creatures? Sometimes human beings see this being done, you know. They see these hairy things, you know, that aren't human and don't seem to be animal, either.

A. Yes, these are the SI's pets, which collect samples from earth for the SI's. Just like we use chimpanzees or porpoises, dogs and cats and horses, etc., to do work for us. But for what purpose they want these samples, I don't really know.

Q. Do they put them back on earth after they get through studying the samples?

A. I don't think so. However, I have read of cases where there would be an exception to this. One not long ago... where a man was out fishing in rowboat and vanished completely... then turned up, clear across the United States in another location, about 5 or 6 years later... with a different mind, and a new wife and family! He couldn't remember his life at all, past the fishing and rowboat. There have been too many similar cases of this sort for it to be an accidental happening. I am sure the SI's "collected" the man, studied him, created a state of amnesia in his mind to protect their interests, and put him back on earth to pick up the threads of a new life, perhaps under a "controlled observation" by them.

Q. Do you think they might have done that so people wouldn't bother him? Like people would, if he told of being kidnapped by flying saucer people?

A. That's an ingenious possibility, but since this case has been repeated, I prefer my own theory about it.

Q. What is their time-span like? Is their time the same as our time?

A. No. Not at all. That is the one big difficulty the SI's have. Their sense of time in this dimension is completely different from ours. They have a great difficulty in figuring out our time as such.

Q. Are your SI's connected with the New Jersey "Devil"?

A. I hadn't heard of that report. Of course, my SI's are different than all the reports of OI's. For instance, they don't have to use knobs and gears and things of that sort in their craft. They think their craft - fly their craft by thought-control. My SI's are much more advanced than other forms of OI's. A different species altogether. Z., the scientist, said that in all his years of experience in studying UFO's, he had never encountered the kind of SI that I was communicating with. And he affirmed, absolutely, that I was communicating with them.

Q. The people you have brought back to life, by signaling the SI's to have them supply their form of other-dimensional power to the injured or dying person - what do their friends and family think of it?

A. Take Mrs. Don Whitehead, of Fort Worth, Texas for instance. All her friends, including her husband and family, thought it was wonderful, or so they told me. The girl in Washington that I saved, through the SI's who was so hopelessly gone before I entered the picture, is alive now and getting along well in West Virginia. As a matter of fact, I had a letter from her mother, not long ago, thanking me again for what I did for her daughter. I just went to her hospital room and used my "secret system" to signal the SI's who streamed their power into her, in her bed. And that healing power grew on her, and saved her. I had to get the permission of her family, the permission of the hospital, the permission of the doctors on the case, and the permission of the police, before I could go into her hospital room to help her. She was dying when I walked into her room. A machine was doing her breathing for her. It took me only 5 minutes to save her life. My daughter, Lornie, went with me, and stood beside me at the time. Although Lornie didn't know what my "secret system" was, I used her to increase my power as a sending-receiving set to the SI's by holding her hand and forming a link with her brain. The girl's name was Brenda Sue P., and although she has not completely recovered to this day, she is alive and consistently progressing, her mother said in her letter to us. And there have been other people I have saved, who were given up as hopeless before I entered the picture. I was allowed to use my "secret system" of the SI's because, as they or their families said, "why not?". Nothing could hurt these dying or hopeless people anyway.

Q. And you brought this Brenda Sue P. back to life?

A. Yes. When I saw her in her hospital room she had tubes running into her head. She was one of the most badly-hurt humans I have ever seen.

Q. These people that you have brought back to life, you say that they are part SI now?

A. Yes, I am sure they are.

Q. Can they switch over to another dimension now that they are part SI?

A. That's a good question. I hadn't thought of that. But I doubt it.

Q. Since they are part SI, like you are... couldn't they communicate with the SI's now, like you do?

A. That's possible. It does give the SI's a foothold, I think, with these people; but of course, whether they could take the SI power and survive, during communication, I don't know.

Q. They would have ESP power now, you mean?

A. Now they will have highly-developed ESP ability, yes. And as they get well, their family and friends will find out they are different people than they were, with different personalities. I am sure of it.

Q. Did God make their dimension, before he made ours?

A. When you say "God", what do you mean?

Q. I guess "God" is a kind of force.

A. That's right. A combination of intelligence and force. And only God knows what God had done, I am sure.

Q. Would "heaven" be in our dimension, or in the SI dimension?

A. "Heaven?" There you go again? "Heaven" is a man-made word, and we don't know what it is. We accept it on faith, from the Bible. My guess would be that when Jesus talked about Heaven, he meant that we are going into a better life. For example, a long time ago, in another life, you might have been a sick cat that was picked up by the police and shot in the head, to put you out of your misery. I just saw that happen tonight, on my way home; and when I saw that poor cat being eliminated, I thought, "There, but for the grace of God, go I." So

Heaven could be a better life for your soul to enter into, when your present body or shell dies. It's possible that if you died tonight, and you had built up a good soul and spirit inside yourself, you might be assigned by the powers-that-be to a different, better world in another dimension, or another planet, where similar improved intelligences have gathered - and this sort of thing keeps progressing into Infinity. Perhaps Jesus knew this, and tried to teach the thought to humans whose minds were too finite to grasp the scope of infinity.

Q. And it might be Heaven, compared to this life in this world?

A. That's right!

Q. But it wouldn't exactly be real Heaven.

A. No. Not at all the way we humans think of Heaven, such as floating in the clouds with Angels, drinking an unlimited supply of beer and playing on harps. Ha!

Q. You have said you think the SI's are what we call "ghosts", such as in the so-called haunted castles in Europe?

A. Yes, I am absolutely positive of it. We have heard ghostly groaning and sighing up in our own apartment. And if you had heard it you would know what I am talking about. It isn't, and couldn't be any human agency. I have read about the ghostly sounds in castles that were haunted, and houses that were haunted, as being low, groaning noises. That's the SI noise. And putting two and two together, since the SI's have been trying to get me over to Europe into one of those isolated castles and stay for a year. I am positive those isolated spooky castles are haunted. They are haunted by UFO's and SI's. They use those isolated castles for bases.

Q. Then why are people sometimes attacked by ghosts? Could it be the evil OI's?

A. It could be my SI's, or it could be the evil OI's taking human form at the time, probably to drive people away, from their base there at the castle. In other words, you go to one of those old, isolated castles, and the SI's want to get you away from their base there. So it takes ghostly form, like a human, and lets your eyes see it.

Q. Do the SI's have anything to do with the cases where people are sometimes burned to death, and where their clothes aren't even scorched?

A. I don't know.

Q. In a book I read, the author says flesh and blood have been seen falling from the sky. Do the SI's have anything to do with this?

A. I don't think the flesh and blood fell from the sky. I think the flesh and blood fell out of the other dimension. In all cases where I have read of a shower of fish or rocks falling from the sky, I believe it is caused by the SI's opening a crack in their dimension to let their craft in or out, and that when they do, it somehow causes this phenomena. It might be that the fish or rocks or flesh and blood might be taken into the other dimension as the SI's go into it, right along or out of the ocean in their craft. They see people on the bank of the lake or the ocean, so they switch off, into another dimension. But as they have come up out of the water their power might draw fish up with them, or rocks, or even people. Then the craft goes into another dimension along with these items. When they switch on again into this dimension, in a different area than before, perhaps clear across the world, then these same fish or rocks or people, or parts of people, come back out with them and shower down.

Q. I read in the papers where two helicopters crashed down in Florida, in the area where you said the SI's had PK'd.

A. Yes. Several years ago the SI's gave a demonstration of their power, asking me to write to the Government in advance, to tell what was going to happen. At that time the Government was holding military exercises in North Carolina and South Carolina, and the SI's said that they would give a demonstration of their power, against these military exercises. Well, you never saw anything like it in your life. Helicopters crashed; planes crashed; all sorts of freak accidents happened; and the area was struck by two hurricanes while the military exercises were in progress, causing tremendous floods in North and South Carolina. It's peculiar, but once an area is PK'd, the power just continues to grow. It does not diminish or pass away. For instance, the SI's gave another demonstration against combined U.S. and Spanish military exercises off the coast of Spain, documented in advance by letters to Government agencies, etc. That is, the SI's had me warn the Government before they struck. And the same things happened: those military exercises had all kinds of freak accidents, such as plane and helicopter crashes, etc. But my point is, the "PK" kept on growing after the military exercises were over, in that area. And later on, in the same area, two of our nuclear planes crashed into each other and we, that is, the U.S., lost some nuclear bombs on the land and in the ocean. It caused an awful flap, if you remember.

Q. Can you remove this PK when you want to?

A. I don't know.

Q. I guess it would take the SI's to remove the PK.

A. I'm sure they could. I have never tried removing it.

Q. Well, it seems to me you sort of act like a spark that starts it. And since you're only the spark that starts it, you couldn't stop it if you wanted to, once it got out of your hands?

A. That's a good question. I might be able to. Being the only human working with my SI's, they place a high value on my wishes. And if our President would cooperate with the SI's, to arrange for them to have a base in the U.S., I am sure the SI's would erase the "PK" that now exists, and grows, in certain areas. Then, if there was any double-crossing by the government, the SI's would replace the PK, many times magnified in power.

Q. You mean, even worse?

A. Ten-fold worse.

Q. How does the PK grow? Do the SI's make it grow stronger? Or is it natural for this strange power to grow by itself?

A. It's just natural. It doesn't need any help, once it begins. This same "PK" was used in ancient ages by the Egyptians, in their burial tombs, and as time went on, the curse, or PK effect they used on the tomb, grew more powerful and virulent, instead of weaker. When Europeans opened the tombs a long time later, the PK, which had been planted there long ago attacked them, silently and invisibly. They couldn't see it, feel it, touch it, smell it, or sense it in any way. Nevertheless, it just attached itself to them, and followed along with them wherever they went, and waited, until the time and circumstances were just right for an accident or an illness. Then, like lightning, the PK made it come to pass, and the persons suffered violent accidents, or illnesses, which killed them or ruined them for life. Thus the explorer was punished, just as the inscription on the door of the tomb that had been violated had warned would happen. I am positive that the SI's made friends with the Egyptians, and taught them how to use PK forms. There are many different kinds and forms of PK, you know.

At least, they taught the Egyptians as much as they felt was safe for the Egyptians to have, at that time. PK grows, you see, just as you would take a package of seeds and plant them, out in a field. Then after a bit, sprouts come up, then shoots and stalks; and after a time there is a whole big field full of tall, powerful PK, just as a corn field grows. But PK is invisible, with the power in it growing, all the time, the power being intelligently directed by the intelligence that started that PK field in the first place. In the case of the Egyptians using PK in their tombs to guard their dead, I believe it was "Tutunkaman" (or something like that) who had a seal put on the door of his crypt, warning people not to enter - that a "curse" would follow anyone who did to their doom. Well, about a dozen or so scientists did break open the door of the crypt, and in the time following, all of them died mysterious violent deaths, wherever they were in the world. Like if the SI's put PK on a person, then that person would be a walking PK plant, intelligently directed, a deadly accident just waiting for the right time to happen.

Q. This PK - doesn't it affect radio waves?

A. It affects everything, yes! I could give you a big, long list of more that 100 different effects that go with the PK. And these over - 100 different effects, or ways, effect the area it is attacking, or helping.

Q. Will the PK you put on my friend, Ida, affect her?

A. That's "rainbow PK", my name for it, for want of a better expression. It gives her an "angel", a sort of an invisible guardian. It's hard to explain it in English, except to tell you that it helps her. It helps her grow and keep her health. Oh, she might get sick or have an accident, but without that PK she might die or get killed. It guards her, and helps her. It's a tremendous force, working inside her and around her and for her.

Q. This PK she has, is it growing on her?

A. Yes. All the time. It's terrific. I have put that same rainbow PK on my entire family, to guard them and keep them well and happy.

Q. Well, now, let's ask about hurricanes. They all seem to start from one section. Is PK starting them?

A. Yes. The SI's start the hurricanes.

Q. How about this year (1967)? Will the SI's start any hurricanes this year (1967)?

A. I make the hurricanes by signaling the SI's. I have already planted the hurricane seeds for this coming season of 1967. I have asked the SI's to produce 3 simultaneous hurricanes this year, which is so rare it's only happened a few times in history, you know. But my best year was several years ago, when I ran three hurricanes across the center of the SI target! Cape Kennedy. The year after that, only one hurricane came up, and it was a dandy - Hurricane Betsy. Betsy did everything I asked her to. She even backed up for me (and remember, I was constantly telling government agencies and scientists in advance what the cane would do next).

Regarding Betsy's backing up, I had tried to get hurricanes to back up the previous year, without succeeding. Betsy was the first. Then, after she backed up like I told her to, I directed her over to the Michoud Space Complex in Louisiana, a secondary target of the SI's. In other words, Hurricane Betsy did everything for me but roll over and play dead. Well, last year I gave a terrific demonstration for Government agencies and scientists, with Hurricane Inez. She did everything I told her to, just like Betsy did. And most of the things I told her to do were in absolute contradiction to what the Hurricane Center at Miami said she'd do. This year, 1967, I am working to get three simultaneous hurricanes which will function just like a football backfield...

Editor's note: In 1967, three simultaneous hurricanes appeared in fact. The occurrence of three simultaneous hurricanes is so rare it has only happened five times in history.

Q. You mean all three at once?

A. Yes, all converging on Cape Kennedy, from different directions.

Q. Will all of them join into one?

A. No, I don't think so, because each hurricane is in a force field, and force fields tend to repel each other.

Q. How do you put these hurricane seeds out? Do you just think them in your mind?

A. I picture the hurricane symbols for the SI's, after contacting the SI's, and they take it from there. They can do it. Once the hurricane appears, I make a crude map showing the SI's where I want the cane to go, and most of the time the cane has followed my map accurately.

Q. I guess if You wanted three hurricanes, the SI's could do it.

A. Oh, yes, They could give me a dozen. But the thing of it is, I don't know whether the SI's would want to or not. It would be an awful hardship on the people, although it would be a good demonstration for the government.

Q. Not as much a hardship as the attack on the U.S. you say will take place within two years by Russia and China.

A. That's right. It would be quite an inconvenience to have a nuclear bomb land in Philadelphia. Ha Ha!

Q. You say that there are three UFO's, each as large as the Earth?

A. Not three but four!

Q. And they are around the earth all the time?

A. I think they either come into position, or they come from another dimension, when they are signaled. I do not know if they stay there around the earth all the time. But when I use the "Emmy-Emma" signal they know what it is, and the four craft come up into position and exert an electromagnetic influence on the earth's spin, causing earthquakes, floods, volcanic eruptions, etc.

Q. Do the SI's control hurricanes?

A. Not long ago I signaled the SI's for an early hurricane, and instead of that, they gave me, within a week or so, 30 tornados stretching out in a line across the Midwest, all at once. They mistook the hurricane symbol I sent them for a tornado attack demonstration. The symbols for the canes and tornados are almost the same.

Q. You don't think it's the Oi's, or evil SI's, then, making the tornados?

A. No. These are my SI's, starting and controlling the tornados. As I explained, when I signaled the SI's for an early hurricane, they took it that I wanted a demonstration of storms, because the symbol I use for them for them for a cane is much like the symbol I use with them for storms. They misunderstood and gave me tornados instead of canes.

Q. You say the SI's might destroy the U.S.? Could you enlarge on that?

A. No, you're wrong, I didn't say that. The SI's will allow Russia and China to destroy us, if we don't cooperate with the SI's. Think of the world as a large field on a farm. If one section of the field won't grow crops, or be productive, then the farmer will just quit planting on it and let it go to rot. And that's what will happen to the U.S. if we don't pay attention to the SI's.

Q. You say the Asians and black will become the big powers in the world, eventually?

A. Yes, that's right. The Asian race will become the main chief power of the world, after the U.S. is destroyed, and the black people will become the second largest power. The Asians will come pouring over the Alaskan straits, incidentally, into this country, to occupy it, after we have been destroyed. And when that happens, the whites will practically be non-existent. If there are any whites left, the Asians and blacks will pursue them and eliminate them, as if they were the plague, because the Asians and blacks have had enough of the whites in this world.

Q. Do you think they will put the whites in colonies by themselves?

A. No. I do not think they will allow the whites to exist, and risk the whites becoming numerous and strong again. I think the whites will be attacked and eliminated in the same way that we attack and eliminate cancer in the body, when we find it.

Q. After the U.S. is destroyed, the SI's will still come down and try to help the world, won't they?

A. No, I don't think so. After the nuclear war that destroys the U.S. the SI's will be so far behind in their plans, it will be pitiful. That's why they put such a high value on me, because I can communicate with the SI's and other humans - the first human to be able to do so since Moses' time. Now, the OI's want this to happen, want us to be destroyed, want the SI's held back, unable to reach an alliance with the human race.

Q. In the end, I guess it just boils down to SI's vs. Oi's, and they are sort of using the earth as a battle field.

A. I think it's more like a game of chess between the several kinds of SI's, and we are the chess pieces. They are too far advanced to shoot at each other or hurt each other, as we do. They think in such dimensions and at such depths, that it would be beyond our tiny, limited minds to even imagine it. But if you compare my SI's to the Oi's, there simply is no comparison. My SI's are vastly superior.

Q. Then the SI's thinking is not limited in scope?

A. No. It is unlimited. Both the SI's and the Oi's know how to contact unlimited intelligence, intelligence from all the ages past, everywhere.

Q. Do you think that they can travel into the past, into the future?

A. Absolutely. They have shown me how to get intelligence from the past ages, myself. They showed me how to "tap" intelligence from the wisdom of the Aztecs, the Mayans, the Incas, and the ancient Egyptians. I have incorporated this knowledge into a book, which I have used in helping people - methods not known or used in this world at all, anywhere else. I call these methods "OD" methods, for "other dimensional". By using these methods I have saved people given up as hopeless by doctors. However, I warn all that I work with, to work closely with their doctors, dentists, etc. that PK and OD methods certainly do not replace our human medicine and surgery and doctors. I explain carefully that UFO intelligences cannot pull teeth, or remove an infected appendix, etc. OD methods are to be used with the doctor's permission only after all regular medicine and surgery have failed. The disk work (see Fate Magazine, December, 1967; Saucer News, Winter Issue, published 1968) is something else, and the above is explained carefully to the "disc people" who receive the charged discs. Incidentally, any human being who needs help of any kind whatsoever, can get this help by sending for a disc charged with power from the UFO's - to Ted Owens, President, The Sotas, Box 17005, Philadelphia, Pa., 19105. There is no charge whatsoever. This is not a commercial enterprise, but an expression of compassion by the SI's for humans, to show their love and affection for humans.

Q. It seems like this PK work and OD work, and the discs, is like the work Jesus did. Could that have been how he brought people back to life?

A. Certainly. I am positive that he knew these OD methods. Either he was a SI, or he had been trained by the SI's. No doubt about it in my mind.

Q. He healed some persons by letting them touch his robe.

A. Yes, but that was like a trick, misdirection. He healed them all right, but he knew that if he tried to explain that he was using an OD method, coming from another dimension, they wouldn't understand him. How much simpler to tell them to touch his robe. He would way, "Now I'm going to rub some spit on your eyelid, and your eye will get well". But while he was rubbing spit on the person's eyelid, he was bringing into play the OD effects which would heal that person. In Texas, some years ago, when I was helping people there, I would tell them to watch a light, and listen to my voice. While they were doing that, I was secretly using OD techniques which the SI's had given me. And believe me, they were helped. But they knew nothing whatsoever about my "secret system", within a system, being used on them. Not that I am comparing my work with that of Jesus, mind you. I would not even begin to compare - I have too many human frailties, faults and weaknesses - but I have discovered all this, seemingly by accident, and do know how to use it. Jesus knew how to use it, and Moses also knew much of this.

Q. How about Jesus' disciples?

A. No. I believe that he tried to train them, but it just didn't work too well. It would be just like me trying to teach you about it, even draw pictures of it, but you still wouldn't be able to grasp it, because these strange symbols aren't like anything to be found in the English language - or anywhere else on earth, for that matter. You take Edgar Cayce, he was a tremendous psychic. He would tell you what was wrong with you, then tell you how to cure it. He did tell others how he did it, even wrote books about it, but when he died, there was no more Edgar Cayce miracle. His son and followers have tried to duplicate Edgar's work, but no human could do so. There was just one Cayce, because only Cayce could "see" what was going on inside his mind. The same is true with me.

Q. Moses had a staff that turned into a snake, didn't he?

A. Yes. I think he told the SI's, "Look, you have got to give me some proof to prove to people that all this is real. People only believe in their physical senses. They don't understand OD effects. My people will tell me I am crazy, so, oh voice in a burning bush, give me something solid to show my people". And the voice in the "burning bush" said, "Very well", and proceeded to show Moses how to use his staff for that purpose. This convinced Moses, first of all, that he wasn't imagining things. And later it helped convince his people.

Q. Moses struck a rock with the staff, and water came out of it.

A. Actually, I don't think it was Moses at all, but the SI's that did it, using the staff action just as Jesus used the "touch robe" technique. Just as with the girl at Lourdes. You know, the SI's have told me they brought about the miracles at Lourdes, and are trying to set up a modern "Lourdes" here in the United States, but can't get any cooperation. (See Winter Issue of Saucer News, 1968.) The SI's knew that the people could believe in a "magic staff", much easier than believing in the SI's.

Q. Can you tell me about some of these things, or miracles as you call them, that the SI's have done - when you have notified government agencies and scientists in advance of these happenings? I believe you said you had 180 cases.

A. Yes. 183 miracles, to be exact, all documented. I'm putting all of that into book form, to follow the first volume. In the first book I will make some references to some of these miracles, and describe them briefly. But in my book, coming out later, and entitled, "I WORKED FOR THE UFO CREATURES", I will go into all these cases in detail. Of course, nothing like this book has ever been written, with the exception of the books of Moses, in the Bible.

How To Contact The Space People

At this point, both of us exhausted with the interview, we concluded. From all this material... the reader can now know the true facts about UFO's never before printed or revealed, and can have an excellent idea of how to go about contacting the UFO's themselves. You have obtained this information from the only living human being who can communicate back and forth with UFO intelligences, AND PROVE IT.

P K MAN (Ted Owens)

Ted Owens

Appendix

Ted Owens

Exhibit A

Pat Shannon
14705 112th NE
Kirkland,
Washington
98033

STATE OF CALIFORNIA)
COUNTY OF LOS ANGELES) ss

TO WHOM IT MAY CONCERN:

Ted Owens made the following predictions. The events so predicted came about within a few days after each prediction. All predictions were made before they actually occurred.

1. He predicted the "1966 East Coast Fireball" which would fly over Philadelphia.
2. He stated there would be an early 1966 hurricane. Hurricane Alma appeared within six days.
3. He predicted in advance a major earthquake in California.
4. He predicted violent lightning in the City of Philadelphia. Three such storms occurred within a few days and weeks.
5. He predicted Communist attack planned against U.S. Warships at Viet Nam. A few days later the Communists tried a sneak attack with torpedo boats.

I declare the above to be a true statement of facts.

ated: August 11, 1966

Patricia Shannon
Notary Public in and for the State of California, County of Los Angeles

EXHIBIT A

13

Pat Shannon
14705 112th NE.
Kirkland Washington 98033

State of California
County of Los Angeles

TO WHOM IT MAY CONCERN:

Ted Owens made the following predictions. The events so predicted came about a few days after each prediction. All predictions were made before they actually occurred.

1. He predicted the "1966 East Coast Fireball" which would fly over Philadelphia.

2. He stated there would be an early 1966 hurricane. Hurricane Alma appeared within six days.

3. He predicted in advance a major earthquake in California.

4. He predicted violent lightning in the City of Philadelphia. Three such storms occurred within a few days and weeks.

5. He predicted Communist attack planned against U.S. Warships at Viet Nam. A few days later Communists tried a sneak attack with torpedo boats.

I declare the above to be a true statement of facts.

Dated: August 11, 1966

Patricia Shannon
Notary Public in and for the
State of California,
County of Los Angeles

Exhibit B

THE FOLLOWING IS A TESTIMONIAL TO THE VALIDITY OF THE PREDICTIONS MADE BY TED OWENS AND SENT TO ME ON THE DATES STATED

MARCH 10, 1966 - End of drought conditions to occur in near future. (By end of June, Udall had made a report to President Johnson stating that the drought had definitely diminished in intensity.

APRIL 26, 1966 - U.F.O. seen over Philadelphia. This was predicted on April 19 in carbon copy sent to me.

JUNE 1, 1966 - Predicted early hurricane. Alma occurred five days later.

JUNE 17, 1966 - Predicted major earthquake in California. Same occurred eleven days later.

JUNE 18, 1966 - Predicted series of violent electrical storms in Philadelphia area. Several fierce storms occurred during the end of June and in July-- unusual amount of lighting.

JUNE 29, 1966 - Warned that U.S. Fleet would be attacked off Viet Nam coast. Two days later, torpedo boats attacked U.S. warships.

OCT. 15, 1966 - Predicted that a U.F.O. would be seen and reported in the mass media, in the vicinity of Philadelphia, on Halloween. The Camden, N.J. newspaper reported a U.F.O. seen by many people on Oct. 31. It was heading for Phila.

Zelda S. Hansell
Zelda S. Hansell
29 S. Wyoming Ave.
Ardmore, Pa. 19003

December 10, 1966

State of Penna.
County of Montgomery

Sworn to before me this 12th day of December 1966.

Maria R. Pavoni
Maria R. Pavoni
Notary Public
My comm. exp. 2/2/69

EXHIBIT B

THE FOLLOWING IS A TESTIMONIAL TO THE VALIDITY OF THE PREDICTIONS MADE BY TED OWENS AND SENT TO ME ON THE DATES STATED

MARCH 10, 1966 - End of drought conditions to occur in near future. (By end of June, Udall had made a report to President Johnson stating that drought had definitely diminished in intensity.

APRIL 26, 1966 - U.F.O. seen over Philadelphia. This was predicted on April 19 in carbon copy sent to me.

JUNE 1, 1966 - Predicted early hurricane. Alma occurred five days later.

JUNE 17, 1966 - Predicted major earthquake in California. Same occurred eleven days later.

JUNE 18, 1966 - Predicted serious of violent electrical storms in Philadelphia area. Several fierce storms occurred during the end of June and in July-- unusual amount of lightning.

JUNE 29, 1966 - Warned that U.S. Fleet would be attacked off Viet Nam coast. Two days later torpedo boats attacked U.S. warships.

OCT 15, 1966 - Predicted that a U.F.O. would be seen and reported in the mass media, in the vicinity of Philadelphia, on Holloween. The Camden N.J. newspaper reported a U.F.O. seen by many people on Oct. 31. It was heading for Phila.

Zelda S. Hansell
29 S. Wyoming Ave.
Ardmore, Pa. 19003

December 10, 1966

State of Penna.
County of Montgomery

Sworn to me this 12th day of December 1966.

Maria R. Pavoni
Notary Public
My comm. exp. 2/2/69

Exhibit C

April 29, 1965, Thursday

Yesterday, Wednesday, April 28, Ted Owens predicted to me that within the next few days:

(1) A large earthquake would strike the West Coast

or

(2) A hurricane would strike Florida.

Today, the day following Ted's prediction, there was a large earthquake on the West Coast.

Mrs. Jeanne Mangels
Mrs. Jeanne Mangels,
Landlord
418 Peabody St., NW
Washington, D. C.

EXHIBIT C

15

Ted Owens

April 29, 1965, Thursday

Yesterday, Wednesday, April 28, Ted Owens predicted to me that within the next few days:

1) A large earthquake would strike the West Coast.

or

2) A hurricane would strike Florida.

Today, the day following Ted's prediction, there WAS a large earthquake on the West Coast.

Mrs. Jeanne Mangels
Landlord
418 Peabody St., NW
Washington, D.C.

Exhibit D

I certify this to be a true and correct statement:

On the night of May 8, 1967, while watching a rainstorm in the company of H. Owens (Ted) from the top of a tall building in downtown Philadelphia...Mr. Owens offered to make lightning strike in any area that I might point out, as a demonstration of a new weather principle he had discovered. So I took him up on it, and pointed to an area squarely in front of our window...the bridge leading to Camden.

In a few moments after Mr. Owens concentrated on making lightning strike the aforementioned bridge...a lightning bolt did in fact strike that area, just to the right of the bridge.

Since we were standing at the top of a tall building, our field of view was very wide and expansive. Therefore the lighting bolt striking the pinpointed area which I had designated, was interesting.

[illegible]

SIDNEY MARGULIES, ESQ.
May 10, 1967

Sworn to and subscribed before me this 10th day of May, 1967.

[illegible]

Notary Public, [illegible], Philadelphia Co.
My Commission Expires July 7, 1969

EXHIBIT D

16

Ted Owens

I certify this to be a true and correct statement:

On the night of May 8, 1967, while watching a rainstorm in the company of H. Owens (Ted) from the top of a tall building in downtown Philadelphia... Mr. Owens offered to make lightning strike in any area that I might point out, as a demonstration of a new weather principle he had discovered. So I took him up on it, and pointed to an area squarely in front of our window... the bridge leading to Camden.

In a few moments after Mr. Owens concentrated on making lightning strike the aforementioned bridge... a lightning bolt did in fact strike that area, just to the right of the bridge.

Since we were standing at the top of a tall building, our field of view was very wide and expansive. Therefore the lightning bolt striking the pinpointed area which I had designated, was interesting.

SIDNEY MARGULIES, ESQ.
May 10, 1967

Sworn to and Au?????ed
before me this 10th day
of May 1967.

Mollie ???hn
Notary Public, Philadelphia, Philadel-Ma Ca.
My commission expires July 7, 1969

Exhibit E

October 3, 1966, Monday

Mr. Rowland Swank, O.S.C.A.R.

Dear Rowland:

Well, I told you Thursday or Friday that I was working to turn Hurricane Inez from going West, to going North, check?

I had to do two things over the weekend...build Inez up to a hurricane again, after she died down to just a storm... then turn her toward Florida.

Enclosed is photostat of today's N.Y. Times map of Inez... and you can see for yourself that, although last week she was coming in on Cuba, going WestXXX and according to the Weather Bureaus was not supposed to come near the U.S. - she changed direction over the weekend just as I was working for her to do, and shot toward the U.S., just shaving Electro. The paper says Inez's gales and storms are kicking hell out of Electro, but she didn't hit Electro head on. I don't know how much of a miss this is, but it certainly isn't much. I guided Inez 1700 miles in on the target. Not a head on hit, but damn good shooting, nevertheless. Don't you agree?

I'm still trying to turn her in left for a head-on hit, because she's alongside...or if she gets out a little, I'll try to repeat Betsy over again.

P K Man (Owens)

EXHIBIT E

17

October 3, 1966, Monday

Mr. Rowland Swank, O.S.C.A.R.

Dear Rowland:

Well, I told you Thursday or Friday that I was working to turn Hurricane Inez from going West, to going North, check?

I had to do two things over the weekend... build Inez up to a hurricane again, after she died down to just a storm... then turn her toward Florida.

Enclosed is a photostat of today's N.Y. Times map of Inez... and you can see for yourself that, although last week she was coming in on Cuba, going WestXXX and according to the Weather Bureaus was not supposed to come near the U.S. - she changed direction over the weekend just as I was working for her to do, and shot toward the U.S., just shaving Electro. The paper says Inez's gales and storms are kicking the hell out of Electro, but she didn't hit Electro head on. I don't know how much of a miss this is, but it certainly isn't much. I guided Inez 1700 miles in on the target. Not a head on hit, but damn good shooting, nevertheless. Don't you agree?

I'm still trying to turn her in left for a head-on hit, because she's alongside... or if she gets out a little, I'll try to repeat Betsy over again.

P K Man (Owens)

Saucer News

SAUCER NEWS

...AL PUBLICATION OF THE SAUCER AND UNEXPLAINED CELESTIAL EVENTS RESEARCH SOCIETY

...DRESS: P.O. BOX 163, FORT LEE, N.J. 07024
...OM 1615, 303 FIFTH AVE., NEW YORK, N.Y. 10016
...NE: MUrray Hill 6-3743

EDITOR:
James W. Moseley

ASSISTANT EDITOR:
John J. Robinson

...tland Street
...nswick, N.J.

6/12/67

Dear Ted:

Many thanks for having the SI's come through with that promised blackout. I am quite certain that this event, and others which "THEY" shall proform before the convention will attract many persons who otherwise would not have come. We are hopeing for a UFO sighting (good one) or landing about 3 days before the start of the convention to build press interest. The closer to New York the better.

Am sorry Jack McKinney wouldn't let Jim Moseley, John Keel or myself mention your prediction on the air on the evening of the blackout. We had hoped to but he thought it best we not mention it. However you have been mentioned by name on the Long John show (Jim Moseley guest) last Friday (June 9th) and on WBAB by yours truely the same day. Will listen to the Ed Harvey show on the 19th. Don't forget to mention the convention if possible. The evening sessions start at 8 p.m. and the afternoon ones as 2 p.m. Jim and I hope you'll be able to make it for atleast the Saturday or Sunday sessions. Dr. Condon of the University of Colorado is flying in for the event; as are other noted officials.

Probably the best boost for you is the fact that the Summer-Convention issue of SAUCER NEWS contains your letter predicting such a blackout before it actually occurred.

To avoid any misunderstanding I am writing this letter on a personal basis and my opinions do not necessarily agree with those of the entire staff of SAUCER NEWS.

With Kindest regards,

Timothy Green Beckley

Managing Editor

53

SAUCER NEWS

OFFICIAL PUBLICATION OF THE SAUCER AND UNEXPLAINED CELESTIAL EVENTS RESEARCH SOCIETY

ADRESS: P.O. BOX 163, FORT LEE, N.J. 07024
? ROOM 1615, 303 FIFTH AVE., NEW YORK, N.Y. 10016
PHONE : MUrray Hill 6-3743

Portland Street
Brunswick N.J.
?

Editor: James W. Mosley
Assistant Editor: John J. Robinson

6/12/67

Dear Ted:

Many thanks for having the SI's come through with that promised blackout. I am quite certain that this event, and others which "THEY" shall proform before the convention will attract many persons who otherwise would not have come. We are hopeing for a UFO sighting (good one) or landing about 3 days before the start of the convention to build press interest. The closer to New York the better.

Am sorry Jack McKinney wouldn't let Jim Moseley, John Keel or myself mention your prediction on the air on the evening of the blackout. We had hoped to but he thought it best we not mention it. However you have been mentioned by name on the Long John show (Jim Moseley guest) last Friday (June 9th) and on WBAB by yours truely the same day. Will listen to the Ed Harvey show on the 19th. Don't forget to mention the convention if possible. The evening sessions start a 8 p.m. and the afternoon ones as 2 p.m. Jim and I hope you'll be able to make it for atleast the Saturday or Sunday sessions. Dr. Condon of the University of Colorado is flying in for the event; as are other noted officials.

Probably the best boost for you is the fact that the Summer -Convention issue of SAUCER NEWS contains your letter precicting such a blackout before it actually occurred.

To avoid any misunderstanding I am writing this letter on a personal basis and my opinions do not necessarily agree with those of the entire staff of SAUCER NEWS.

With Kindest regards,
Timothy Green Beckley
Managing Editor

Afterword

As this book was in final editorial production I was advised by the SI's that each copy will be coded (charged) so that whoever reads it will activate power from another dimension, placing the reader en rapport with the SI's.

The Author

www.ingramcontent.com/pod-product-compliance
Lightning Source LLC
LaVergne TN
LVHW061243100826
845148LV00008B/1015
* 9 7 8 1 6 0 6 1 1 0 0 1 0 *